Realizing Change

Vipassana Meditation in Action

by

Ian Hetherington

Vipassana Research Publications • Seattle

VIPASSANA RESEARCH PUBLICATIONS
(AN IMPRINT OF)
PARIYATTI®
P.O. BOX 15926
SEATTLE, WA 98115
WWW.PARIYATTI.COM

First edition, 2003

ISBN 1-928706-21-5

Library of Congress Control Number: 2002112313

Photography on pages 2, 18, 32, 60, 80, 130, 148, 172 by Kirk
Brown. © 2003Kirk Brown
Photography on pages 108, 202,224, 238 by Michael Green.
© 2003 Michael Green

Cover design by   www.coolillustrations.com

Printed in Canada

Realizing Change

Contents

PREFACE

Despite the greater availability of meditation courses in recent times, the term Vipassana meditation and its potential remain largely unknown in the West. This book, featuring accounts by practitioners leading everyday lives, aims to make Vipassana both better known and more clearly understood.

Two decades back, I had the good fortune to learn the technique of Vipassana directly from S.N. Goenka, a modern lay meditation master in a tradition dating back to the time of the Buddha. Since then, like countless others, I have come to appreciate what a priceless gift Vipassana is. I know through my own experience, personally and professionally, that the benefits I have received from this meditation practice today are indeed enormous. I am profoundly indebted to Mr. Goenka, whose teaching suffuses this book, and who is a tireless and exemplary ambassador for Vipassana around the globe.

Realizing Change has been five years in the making. Many people worldwide have generously given their time, energy and skill to helping the project come to fruition. I am particularly grateful to the dozens of meditators—students and teachers—who submitted stories about their own experience of Vipassana. It has only been possible to include a sample here. In making this compilation, I have also been fortunate to have a wealth of existing source material in different media to draw upon: the Vipassana Research Institute (India) and Pariyatti (USA) and their authors for an extensive list of books, articles and seminar papers; Karuna Films, filmmakers David Donnenfield, Michael Norton and Gerald Frape and transcribers for scripts and camera interviews; Michael Green and Kirk Brown for photographic images; Paul Fleischman for permission to excerpt from *Cultivating Inner Peace.*

My job has been more anthologist, than originator—to weave personal narratives into a straightforward account of Vipassana meditation and its relevance to contemporary life. Special thanks to editors Rick Crutcher of Pariyatti and to Bill Hart for their perceptive comments, suggestions and patient guidance. By repeatedly driving us back to the basics their advice undoubtedly improved the text. Thanks too are due to the U.K. Vipassana Trust for invaluable access to staff and facilities at the Hereford meditation center.

Friends Kirk and Reinette Brown and my wife Shelina also read everything and were unfailingly encouraging—the ideal support team.

Vipassana has been a central part of my life for the past twenty-four years and the text naturally reflects my own experience and understanding, both as a meditator and in my role as an assistant teacher. Where there are shortcomings, they are mine alone and no reflection on the teaching, which is flawless.

Deepest thanks to all who have contributed to this joyful work. May its merits be shared with every one of them.

Herefordshire, UK
2002

INTRODUCTION

Where to now?

Hurricane-force changes characterize the times. Forever raising or dashing our fortunes, they test us to the limit. Is there shelter in the storm? The world won't stop to let us off, so what to do and which route to go? Do we bend or break? Vipassana is a practice of experiencing change—face to face with full understanding—moment by moment throughout our days. By realizing change—face to face with full understanding—we can be doers rather than done-tos. The aim of this book is to introduce Vipassana meditation as a tried and tested way of solving our everyday problems.

The book is written both as celebration and invitation; a celebration of a living tradition of meditation which is being practiced around the world today, positively transforming people's lives in great ways and small, as it has unfailingly for over two thousand years; an invitation to journey together into a fascinating realm of feeling, thought and action.

Vipassana is an ancient meditation technique of India. The Buddha discovered it, attained full enlightenment using it and made it the essence of his teaching, which spread throughout the Indian subcontinent and then on to neighboring countries. For five hundred years Vipassana flourished in India but then eventually it became polluted and was lost there.

However in Burma (now Myanmar) a chain of devoted teachers maintained the theory and the practice of the technique in its original form over the centuries. Sayagyi U Ba

Khin, a respected lay meditation teacher and high government official, was the person directly responsible for relaunching Vipassana in the modern era. At his center in Rangoon he taught foreigners as well as native Burmese. Among his closest students was SN Goenka, a Burmese businessman of Indian origin whose family had settled in Myanmar some generations before. In 1969, after fourteen years studying meditation and assisting his teacher, Mr Goenka returned to India. The mission entrusted to him by U Ba Khin was to take Vipassana back to its birthplace, the land of the Buddha, and from there to spread it around the world. Accordingly Mr Goenka started to give courses in Vipassana, first in India and then abroad. In time, meditation centers exclusively devoted to the teaching were established.

Although Vipassana has its origin in India and has been preserved in the Buddhist tradition, it contains nothing of a sectarian nature and can be accepted and applied by people of any background. In the West people often feel uneasy at the mention of meditation. Various negative associations are made: with "cults;" with "other religions;" with "mysticism." In sum, people often feel about meditation, "This is not for us." By its progress over the past thirty years Vipassana has shown how unfounded these anxieties are. The approach is practical, rational and scientific—an objective investigation of our own minds and bodies, free from any ritual or blind belief. Members of all religions and none, coming from every part of the world and every walk of life, are successfully practicing Vipassana. This should come as no surprise. Our problems are universal and the solution must likewise be universal. Now, as in the past, people of East and West are ultimately the same. Tangible evidence of the technique's effectiveness is offered here in anecdote and research. Through the practice of Vipassana and across all cultural boundaries, we will see how individuals are not only developing their own potential as human beings but are able to make a greater contribution to society as a whole.

The invitation, dear reader, is this. You'll find an outline description of the technique in these pages so that you know what's involved. However the book is not a do-it-yourself meditation manual and shouldn't be used as such. There's no substitute for learning Vipassana by your own personal experience. For this you need to undertake a ten-day course with an authorized teacher in a supportive environment. These courses are designed so that you can discover first-hand how to meditate and get the best results.

Alongside the account of the technique is a sampling of the voices of meditators from different communities: young and old, female and male, simple and sophisticated. Some contributors' names have been altered by request. Each has his or her own story—how they came to Vipassana, what they've learned, the struggles, the gains; all humanity at the water's edge, finding common refreshment in a practice focused on peace, happiness, compassion and loving kindness. This is the terrain we'll be travelling.

The book is arranged in three parts:

Section A: "Vipassana—Meditating on Change" looks at the impact of change on our lives today, what Vipassana meditation is and what happens on a ten-day course.

Section B: "Vipassana—Changing Everyday Life" describes the various ways that individuals and organizations are applying the teaching in everyday situations, at home, with friends and in settings such as education, business and administration, social reform and health.

Appendices provide information for those wanting to find out more about Vipassana and how to set about joining a course.

May what you read here give encouragement and direction to your own search for happiness and truth.

VIPASSANA — MEDITATING ON CHANGE

Chapter 1

CHALLENGE and CHANGE

Conceived out of wedlock in a small coastal village in Greece around 1965, my birth mother was unable to keep and raise me in the cultural climate of that place and time. I was, instead, placed in a nearby orphanage after my delivery on the outbound village bus. These were rather inauspicious beginnings, yet at six months I was adopted by a Greek-American family and brought to the States, to a large city in the Midwest. My family provided a great deal of care that stabilized and grounded me during my formative years.

The wounds of adoption history, for both family and son however were never directly addressed, leaving some of these to fester. Also, some strange family dynamics added salt to such wounds, and I was left with the task of making sense of all the caring and love experienced in my family against a constant buzz of internal anxiety and discomfort. In childhood, I addressed this challenge as many kids do, by engaging their moms in philosophical conversations. To this day I remember many of these conversations, the center of which was my preoccupation with the origin of life, the end of life, and the suffering of others.

After an Ivy League education and a master's degree in spirituality, I returned to my hometown and took a job in a local "progressive age" bookstore to read all I could about the human condition. My formal education didn't satisfy my existential curiosity, and my intention in taking this job, along with making a small bit of money, was to explore the ironies within this universal condition and within my own story as well. I read books on healing, family dynamics, adoption, grief, the "new science," etc. Finally I made my way to the section on Buddhism, and the message I gleaned from one author in particular was that in order to transcend suffering, one must first transcend the field of thought and language. At this point, one reaches a dual perspective where both the beauty and the madness of life disappear into one silent mystery. According to this author, understanding and reading alone cannot resolve this paradox; only meditation can do so.

Meditation it would then be, and off I went to learn the way beyond suffering . . . .

> —*Dimitri Topitzes, from Wisconsin USA,*
> *sat his first Vipassana course in 1996.*

Change—the only certainty there is

For those raised in prosperity towards the end of the twentieth century, we might feel entitled to think that most of life's problems have been solved. The majority of the population eats well and has a comfortable home. We live longer, spend less of our time in paid employment. We have more money than ever before and a wide range of goods and services to purchase and enjoy. And yet, if suicide rates, divorce statistics and drug and alcohol abuse figures are reliable indicators, even the affluent are not happy. Not surprisingly the various minorities, ethnic groups in their ghettos, the elderly, the disabled or sick, the unemployed underclass—all who lack access to wealth and opportunity, do worse on every count. A cycle of deprivation easily becomes rooted which is naturally followed by bitter consequences not only for the individual but, indirectly, for everyone. The same cities which are financial and trading dynamos during the day, become destitute shelters by night. Scenes we would like to link with distant shanties are happening now in our own back yards.

Half the world seems busy beyond belief, working all hours, burning out. The other half is unoccupied, disengaged from the action, resentful. What kind of hellish scheme is this?

In the developing countries the simple necessities of grain, water and shelter cannot be assumed, despite the planet's abundant wealth. There is a danger that many emerging nations will rush headlong into Western-style "progress," superimposing fresh divisions on their own populations. Poverty, if not absolute, certainly remains a relative condition, when compared with the living standards of the industrialized world. As ever, survival is a full time occupation for most in these parts of the globe. However they, in their turn, might be surprised to discover that the riches that many crave have failed to bring contentment. The price of economic success is high, not only for the obvious losers but also for the seeming winners. Fewer workers in factories, farms, offices and shops work longer hours with increased duties, frequently for less pay and little satisfaction. The impact of the quantity and quality of change on people's lives is everywhere to be seen. A secure job is fast becoming a thing of the past along with the welfare safety net that often underpinned it.

Today's schedule—the appointments, the tasks, the chores, priorities, deadlines. Personal time? Blanked out.

Designer dreams are relentlessly manufactured and marketed for every segment of the population. Those who work hard find themselves driven to play hard too—in the gym, the bar or club, along the shopping mall. The pressure to achieve and display success is uppermost and where there are insufficient prizes, or greed dominates, crime and corruption thrive. The menu of escape routes, such as partying, gormandizing, bingeing, exotic travel, acquiring state of the art this or that, is often sampled. However the relief these tidbits offer is temporary; a momentary distraction from the daily grind. Where is this taking us?

Sex selling everything from cars and cosmetics to sport and bread loaves—an epidemic obsession.

What can we say about the process of change we are living through? Life has always involved struggle but for pace and intensity this age is probably unmatched in human history. The revolutions in science, technology, medicine and communications grab one set of headlines. The waves of competing ideologies give a different slant: colonialism; capitalism; fascism; communism; racism; feminism; environmentalism; fundamentalism; the list keeps growing. But it's at the human level that the dramas play and the fallout is felt. So many questions are raised, either to be ignored or met with a vacuum where the answers should be. Tradition buckles in the face of modernity. If there is no work, what are we to do? If it feels good, do it—forget the consequences. When the going gets tough, the tough get going! Is there any remaining bond with partner, parents, children, friends, workmates, business associates and you, my neighbor? Beyond the niceties, is there anything apart from naked self interest? Everywhere money and the gratification of self threaten to displace an intricate web of mutual respect, care and responsibility, which has evolved along with the species. The family, it is said, is dead, religion an irrelevance, politics—the ultimate sham. The cynicism of the times is corrosive and everyone is touched by it. Look no further than hatred-inspired attacks on foreigners or the latest episode of road-rage. We are not in good shape.

Who needs the hassle?

Within this whirlpool, individuals the world over try to make sense of their upturned lives. If we are fortunate, we find the resources within ourselves and the skill and support outside to carry us forward. If we are less lucky, the combination of personal weakness, neglect and aggressive commercialism puts us at risk. Little wonder, without preparation or backup, that so many people suffer from debilitating stress, in one form or another. Stress—our side of the devil's bargain, the flip side of our glitzy culture, a culture in danger of losing touch with its moorings.

Bodies sunbake on a beach
like compulsive smokers
knowing the risk
thinking it'll happen to someone else.

As many are increasingly coming to recognize, something has to be done to regain and sustain balance within society as we proceed through a period of continuing, even accelerating, turbulence. Turning the clock back is not an option, the good old days have gone, their fate to be recorded as quaint items on historical websites. Institutions, schools, business corporations, even governments, can move with the times but only as fast as individuals allow. The key to happiness lies within the individuals themselves.

How does a human being deal with the scale of changes we have been cataloging? Survival—by fighting, fleeing or any other means—requires adaptation. To the extent that we can accept a fresh set of circumstances and modify our behavior accordingly, the more in-tune with the new situation we will be. However, we may perceive many external changes as unwelcome, uncomfortable, upsetting to our established pattern of life and so the response is either one of denial or resistance. On the other hand, we may think we're facing the challenge and coping fine, when, at the deep subconscious level of the mind, intense reaction is going on and our true feelings are being suppressed.

The world may change;
just let me be.

The mind and its contents are all-important. Like an iceberg where only the tip is visible, the conscious mind represents just a small part of the totality. The intellect, the rational portion of the mind, is frequently mistaken for the whole. In fact there is a vast store of unseen and unfelt experience and emotion beneath the surface which is constantly impacting on the conscious mind and over-powering it. To deal with change in anything but a superficial way we need to have full access to the mysteries of our minds. We also need a way of working on ourselves which is safe and will help us to align ourselves, at the depth of our being, with the flux taking place in the universe. Vipassana meditation provides just such a technique. By self-observation each of us can learn the truth about ourselves and develop the living wisdom to manage change effectively.

It was April 26, 1977, almost three years after my time in India and many months since my last formal meditation. Somehow, despite being disoriented in the strange dark Guatemalan streets, I arrived at the airport in time for the flight. My destination was Tikal, site of the largest Mayan ruin. Takeoff however was delayed for quite a while. The city is high and we began a descent to a coastal town where we would stop before reaching Tikal. The aircraft had two engines, but one began to malfunction and we attempted to return to Guatemala City. The plane did not have enough power to fly on one engine and we dropped closer and closer to the ground. I did not know anything was really wrong and I kept looking out my window expecting to see the edge of an airstrip appear. Then we struck something and I knew we were crashing. I quite literally said to myself, "The odds of my surviving this are not very good" and I cradled my head against the back of the seat ahead of me, awaiting the crunch which would end my life. I felt no fear or regret at being in this situation. I felt no positive emotion either. Now it was just an unfolding experience and emotion was not a part of it. We bounced along in a somewhat rough manner but eventually came to a halt. My head came up and so did that of all of the rest of the passengers, everyone looking around with a surprised expression on their face. I could smell smoke, but I was still not concerned. I was in the back part of the plane and I stood at my place while those further behind passed down the aisle towards the exits over the wings. A similar procession was happening from the front of the plane. The last person from the front went out the exit over one wing as I went out the other and now the plane was completely empty. On emerging I ran just far enough to where I thought I would not be caught in any explosion. Then I stopped, turned, and took the first two pictures of a series. Then I retreated further and watched as flames burned higher and higher, a sound like "whump" occurring as each new source of fuel began to contribute to the fire. My things were in the plane, some of them recent purchases and some of them with me from several years of travelling. I felt no regret in knowing they were gone. All told, it was just a very interesting experience.

—Charles Brown attended his first course in 1974.
He now lives and works in Seattle, USA

Some people are looking out and listening for a new direction, like birds waiting for the season's call. They have the strength to explore unknown territory for themselves— what to do next, where to go, in relationships, in their consciences. They experiment with situations, test themselves and their reactions. Articulated or not, a search for self is taking place, a spiritual journey undertaken. Others may be armchair self-developers; when they read or hear about gaining increased control over one's life they feel attracted, yet they are more comfortable with the idea of change than in making the effort to bring it about. Maybe they doubt they can alter the habits of a lifetime or worry about what happens if they do. They may lack confidence that ordinary human beings, rather than some external force, have the capacity to transform their own lives. Above all, they fear the unknown. Another group, ostrich-like, appear more or less satisfied with their existence as it is and show no interest beyond satisfying immediate material needs.

Perhaps these stereotypes are less like fixed personality types than phases anyone can pass through anytime. Tectonic plates keep shifting and so too do the masks we wear. Even the narrowest self-satisfied view of life can be blown apart by a sudden crisis: the death of a loved one, serious illness, losing our possessions or status. Paradoxically it's when we are most vulnerable, wrestling with all the baggage of the past, that we can be most innovative, reaching out for that turning-point. Big or small, immediate or distant, these challenges to our established routines keep flaring up. And if we lack an effective means of dealing with them, they will overpower us now and haunt us later. We pride ourselves today on the technology of space probes, genetic engineering, smart weapons—so often overlooking the need to harness the immense power of our own minds. A power for good to clear our own confusion in a world of hard choices; a chance for real self-improvement—which will help others also. This is the promise of Vipassana meditation.

Everyone wants peace and happiness,
but where do you find them?

Chapter 2

WHAT IS VIPASSANA MEDITATION?

ॐ

I took my first Vipassana course in October 1991. Previously, I had been a shy and nervous person, afraid of meeting new people, and very easily upset. I was also quite a negative person. As a child, I used to be called Eeyore (a doleful donkey character in A.A. Milne's "Winnie the Pooh" stories) because of my glum attitude to life. It must have had some truth in it because independently I was given the same nickname by my peers when I went to university. To some extent I am of course that same person today, but there have been some big changes . . . .
            —*Kerry Jacobs became writer in residence at a*
                        British prison and now teaches in Japan.

Why meditate?

Meditation means different things to different people. In the West the word commonly carries a very loose meaning connected with "thinking things through," "pondering," "reflecting." It can also have associations with prayer or religious contemplation, relaxation and altered states of consciousness. Interest in "meditation" has been growing steadily since the 1960s but the breadth of definition can be confusing. It covers such a range of activities which use the same term in very different ways. To lots of people it remains a hazy area, even weird. What's it all about?

11

In Vipassana, meditation means mental development. It refers to certain specific exercises and techniques which are used for focusing and unknotting the mind.

There are so many other pressing demands on our time and attention. So why would anyone want to meditate?

- With Vipassana we learn how to go inside our hearts and minds for real, to find out who we are and build on that truth.

- We learn how to step back from the world of stimulation outside to ground ourselves, to pull ourselves together—physically, mentally, emotionally, spiritually and reconnect ourselves with nature.

- We learn that peace is inside us and how to find it.

- We meditate to strengthen the mind. An athlete spends hours each day keeping the body fit. The exercises we practice in Vipassana make for a thorough mental workout.

- We heighten our powers of concentration.

- We discover fresh resources of energy.

- We become more available to other people and useful to society.

- We learn a practical way of overcoming the storms and stress in our daily lives.

- We stop creating pain for ourselves and offloading our distress onto others.

- We learn how to develop and share selfless love and compassion.

- We learn how to detoxify the mind, becoming more positive, less reactive; more understanding, less judgmental; more giving and less selfcentered.

- We start to take control, to enrich our lives immeasurably, to change ourselves for the better.

What Vipassana Isn't

Doubt and suspicion often accompany something new, which is what Vipassana meditation is to many. It's healthy to be skeptical—the spiritual field has had its share of frauds, scandals, and even tragedies in recent years. Let us deal with a number of possible misunderstandings directly.

- Vipassana is not about escaping from the demands and responsibilities of the real world. Exactly the opposite: the meditation practice helps to enlarge our capacity for creative participation in society and is rightly called "the art of living."

- Is this another abstract philosophy to be endlessly debated by people in ivory towers? No, the teaching is simple and practical. Everyone, from youngster to professor, can understand it. It is firmly based in our own experience as we learn to observe the truth inside. We are not told what to think, we are shown what we are and can be.

- So what is the aim of Vipassana—to control people, like some religion or sect? Let's be clear about the goal of the technique, which is to purify the mind. As we've already said, mind matters most in a person. It is the engine that drives all we say and do. The human mind is full of goodness, we see it in the innocence of young children, in the outpouring of support for humanitarian aid programs, in moments of self-sacrifice. Unfortunately this positivity is frequently overshadowed by powerful mental impurities such as anger, hatred, passion and fear. Unless we can find a way to root out and release these negativities they will remain the dominant side of our nature. Vipassana helps us to clean up our act. The aim of the technique is control over ourselves, not the manipulation of others.

• So where does enlightenment fit in? Enlightenment is another way of describing the same process and follows naturally. We purify the mind by meditating and doing our best to follow a wholesome lifestyle. Little by little we develop the qualities of enlightenment in us. Vipassana gives good results here and now. That doesn't mean we become instant Buddhas. Slowly but surely changes will show in our attitudes and behavior which ultimately lead to perfection. But let's not get hung up on that one—better look after the pennies and the pounds will look after themselves; heaven can wait!

• So what's the role of the teacher and how is it all financed? A Vipassana teacher or assistant teacher is an experienced meditator whose job it is to guide others in meditation. The aim is to develop understanding and self-sufficiency in those who want to practice, not dependency. He or she is a spiritual friend to the student, not some distant guru. This is a voluntary, unpaid service. Vipassana in this tradition is entirely free of commercialism and has no connection with political or religious organizations.

It was my great good fortune to have been born deeply depressed. My earliest memories are of feeling alone, outcast from other children, sad. In school, for a time I was thought to be developmentally delayed, or "retarded" as the term was in those days. As I grew older, I became even less functional in life, having few friends, spending most of my time alone, being required to repeat seventh grade.

As I entered my teens, and on into my early adulthood, feelings of worthlessness increased and thoughts of suicide plagued me frequently. I sought the help of a long series of psychoanalysts, psychiatrists, psychologists, counsellors and social workers. They were of little help. I was always aware of feeling squeezed into some sort of box constructed of one theory or another. Often, I felt the therapist's ego so strongly intruding into the process that I felt I had become lost in either their own grandiosity or their self doubt.

At this point, in my early twenties, I felt I had reached the end of my rope. Nothing that our mental health professionals could offer seemed to help. I realized that if I were to get to the bottom of my misery, I would have to find the answer myself. I began to wonder about spiritual and religious practices. After all, if so many billions of people all around the world were involved, there must be some benefit, and some common experience.

I began reading from Christianity, Taoism, Vedanta, Confucianism, Zen, Tibetan Buddhism, Sufism, and multiple "New Age" sources. Eventually I tried various practices. I had some hope that perhaps here lay a solution. There seemed to be some common core of truth. In practice, I could not find it. It all seemed buried in layers of ritual, imagery, financial entanglements and even immorality on the part of students and an occasional teacher. The seed of hope remained however, and I gradually developed four rules of thumb to help me in my search:

1. The practice had to be free. If there is knowledge that leads to happiness and freedom, anyone who had found it, anyone who was teaching it would have to want everyone to share it, and would have no use for making a profit from it, while withholding it from those who could not pay.

2. There had to be no leap of faith required, no invisible God, no blind worship. Each step must be clear and acceptable from the start.

3. There could be no exclusion of anyone, and no damnation of those who were of a different path.

4. The teacher must be following his own teaching, and must be free from the taints of immoral action.

These criteria very much sped up my search, but eliminated virtually everything that I had come into contact with so far. I was practicing in a rather eclectic, diluted school of Buddhism when I finally met someone who had taken a course of Vipassana in India.

After I took my first course with Mr Goenka I knew I had found the tool that met all my four criteria for a pure practice! There were no miracles, but I found that, course after course, year after year, my lifelong depression became manageable. More precisely, I became less reactive to the suffering that is the nature of life. Of course, dark moods still come, but they are more like watching a cloud pass in front of the sun than like being buried in a mudslide.

—Ben Turner is a nurse practitioner who has worked on the medical staff of a US jail for nine years.

What is Vipassana?

A man may conquer a million men in battle, but one who conquers himself is indeed, the greatest victor.

—Dhammapada,103

Vipassana meditation is a straightforward, practical way to achieve real peace of mind and to lead a happy, useful life. In Pāli, the old language of India, "Vipassana" means to see things in a special way—that is, as they really are, not just as they seem to be. It is a logical process of mental purification through self-observation.

Vipassana is the technique the Buddha practiced to become enlightened and what he taught for the remaining forty-five years of his life. By direct personal experience the Buddha realized the extent to which we human beings live in a contrived world of fantasy and delusion, our own little world far away from actuality. Vipassana meditation keeps us on track by always focusing on the reality of the present moment.

Vipassana is a universal technique, a way of knowing oneself which is totally nonsectarian, without any unquestioning faith or connection with organized religion. The Buddha did not coin the term "Buddhist," nor did he claim that the path he was teaching was his discovery alone. He had no interest in building up a sect of dependent disciples or establishing a personal following. The central issues for him were twofold: the truth of suffering, physical and mental, and how to fully liberate oneself from this universal condition. "Dhamma," the law of nature operating in and outside us, was what he taught. The whole teaching can be summarized in a few short lines:

Abstain from all unwholesome actions,
Perform wholesome ones,
Purify your mind.

—Dhammapada, 183

The practice of Vipassana meditation is anchored around these three trainings—to avoid unwholesome action, to achieve control over the mind in the service of wholesome actions, to purify the mind through the wisdom of insight. By learning the technique and applying it in life one is not going through some rite or ritual—immediate concrete improvements will result. Now as in the Buddha's time, ordinary men and women as well as those devoted to a spiritual life from many different traditions, benefit from the practice. The shared aspiration, the enduring aim, is to become a better person.

To learn the technique, it is necessary to take a ten-day residential course with a qualified teacher before practicing on one's own. The course, whether it is held at one of the many centers around the world or at some rented site, is always provided on a donation-only basis. There are no charges for the teaching, food or accommodation. The teachers and workers who staff the course all give their services freely. In this pure tradition, all costs are met by the donations of grateful students who have themselves experienced the benefits of the technique and want others to have the same opportunity.

Chapter 3

THE COURSE EXPERIENCE—BEFORE

Students start arriving mid-afternoon. Some stroll down the lane with one small bag, having hitched a ride or taken a bus. Others unload a mound of bedding, suitcases and sitting cushions from their cars. "Welcome to the Vipassana Meditation Center." There is an air of anticipation as they check in and complete their course registration forms. They find their accommodation, unpack their belongings, for this very special ten days. There will be a light meal in the early evening and the course is due to begin about 8:00 p.m. Plenty of time then to walk around the site, get their bearings, to investigate the bathrooms, dining rooms, walking areas and the way to the meditation hall where they will spend much of the next week and a half. Time to reread the course information material and remind themselves of the daily timetable. Maybe a question or two come to mind to ask the organizers before the course gets started.

Some of these students have travelled thousands of miles to attend this retreat; how did they come to be here? Was it a personal recommendation from a family member or friend, was it a book, magazine article, film, or perhaps some chance event?

Migraine was what brought S.N. Goenka to Vipassana. By his mid-twenties, Goenka was already a highly successful businessman and a leader of the Indian community in Burma. However success had brought with it "a lot of tension, a lot of ego" and he began to suffer from severe headaches requiring morphine treatment for the pain. Despite consulting the best doctors around the world, he could not find a cure for his condition. There was a real danger that if he continued with his treatment he would become a morphine addict. Then a good friend, sensing that Goenka's illness was psychosomatic, suggested he take a meditation retreat with Sayagyi U Ba Khin who, as well as being a lay meditation master, also held high government office as Accountant General of the country.

Goenka was attracted but there were some hurdles to overcome. Could meditation really succeed where the cream of the medical profession had failed? And then he feared that he would be required to convert to Buddhism, while he belonged to a strict Hindu family. A meeting with U Ba Khin helped overcome these reservations and convinced Goenka to give the technique a trial. But a shock was in store for him. When he explained that it was because of his headaches that he wished to learn Vipassana, U Ba Khin refused to accept him as a student. Only if Goenka was willing to work according to the technique for purification of mind, prepared to accept any physical improvements as by products of a deeper process, could he join the course. Deeply affected by his teacher's kindness and wisdom, Goenka agreed to work as instructed and even after one course the changes in him were dramatic.

❧

Tony White gave up his job as a London-based health professional in 1995 and travelled to India to go backpacking. He did this to find out more about himself, the world and different cultures and to experience some freedom for possibly the first time in his life.

I was 29 years old and quite dissatisfied with my life. I would have long periods of being low in mood (and had experienced these states for as long as I could remember).

I had just come out of a long and painful relationship. I drank too much alcohol, smoked tobacco and cannabis and occasionally "dabbled" in other drugs such as LSD and "speed." I tried everything I could think of to become at peace with myself and to be happy—from working hard, to getting very intoxicated in my free time, to having a lot of sex with a number of different women. It did not seem to matter what I did, I still had this emptiness, a sadness and dissatisfaction, and the more I tried to achieve happiness the worse I felt.

I had been working as a psychiatric nurse on an acute admissions ward for four years (and prior to this in other psychiatric hospitals for seven years) and I felt really "burned out," as though I had given all I could to the patients and the job and I just couldn't give any more. I felt like a burden to the ward.

So my idea was to travel to India and find the "mysteries of Asia." I had been doing Transcendental Meditation for two to three years but with limited success . . . .

Along with a couple of other Western travellers who were interested in learning the technique, we set off from Udaipur on a long, dusty, tiring and uncomfortable journey to Bhuj in Gujarat, and the Vipassana center where a course was soon to begin.

I was so taken by the thought of doing the course that I arrived at the center with only thirty-five rupees, totally unsure as to how I could get back to Delhi . . . .

—*Tony White, UK*

🐾

Two weeks after their wedding in September 1981, Tim and Karen Donovan set off from the USA on a bicycle trip that eventually led them through Europe and India to the lakeside city of Pokhara in Nepal.

After a couple of days, we stored our bicycles with an innkeeper and rented trekking gear. We set out on a three week trek and walked up to the small village of Muktinath. During this time, the tension increased between us.

Although we were realizing our shared dream of trekking in the Himalaya, we argued and cried our way through beautiful rhododendron forests, spectacular mountain views and strenuous climbs up endless mountain trails. One memorable time, we stopped to take in the spectacular view of the Anapurna range, attempting to be present with the awesome expanse of mountains sparkling white against the brilliant blue sky. We felt helpless. We could not fully appreciate the beauty because our minds were clouded with suffering, emotions and thoughts.

It was in Gorepani, at a little travellers' lodge, that we met a German woman who gave us the information that changed the course of our trip and our lives. We were talking to her about a book on Zen that we had read and how we were attracted to the teachings of the Buddha. We mentioned that we had heard about a man named Goenka who taught Vipassana courses free of charge. She brightened up and said, "I just finished a course with him in Calcutta last month and he'll be going to Kathmandu to teach a course in early May." Tim and I were both thrilled at the news. We could easily finish our trek and be in Kathmandu by that time . . . .

—*Karen Donovan, USA*

My religious background and upbringing always stressed how I should live and conduct my life. In other words I knew intellectually how I should be acting but something inside me didn't always cooperate. Ever since I can remember I've been searching for something to change me inside; so I could be the way I knew I should be without the constant battle within to do what was easier or most pleasant.

In 1988 while on vacation with my wife near Myrtle Beach, South Carolina, I was browsing in a used book store and happened to come across a copy of William Hart's book "The Art of Living." Since it was used and cost only $2.95 I bought it and thought I'd eventually read it. When I did a couple of months later I knew I had to take the ten-day Vipassana meditation course and I felt even before taking it that this is what I had been searching for. One of the things that really impressed me was there was no charge for the course. It was strictly up to you to give if you wish following the course. What ulterior motive could there be with this kind offer?

I took my first course in March, 1989 in Shelburne Falls, Massachusetts and it was the most important thing I've ever done in my life.

—*Ray Goss is a sports broadcaster in Pennsylvania,*
USA. He is married with seven children.

I've been feeling for the last couple of years that I'm going through a change and that I need to go through a change and that some major change is coming up or I'm in the throes of it, which is making life unbearable as it is . . . And I said I really needed to clear my mind and my friend said—"Vipassana meditation," you see. And I thought, there it is, that word again. And so that's when I wrote off for the information, applied, and here I am . . . .

—*Precourse interview with first-time student,*
Australia 1990

Thanda Win is a 34 year old female engineer, working as a Project Manager in Bangkok, Thailand.

The word Vipassana is not strange for us since I belong to a very traditional Burmese Buddhist family. I consider myself a very devoted Buddhist and I started my Vipassana practice at the age of 16 in one of the monasteries in Rangoon, Burma. Whenever I was free I wanted to spend my time in a Dhamma center. I did it almost every year. But I experienced no change in my state of mind. I was as short tempered as I was before and losing the balance of my mind most of the time. I was a very emotional person and I remember my mother used to say, "You work very seriously doing meditation in the course but whenever you come out you don't change at all. If you know Dhamma, why don't you apply it to reduce your anger!" I felt really defeated, I knew that it was not good, but I did not know how to change.

Being away from my home country, and studying and working here in Bangkok, I had no place and no facility to practice Dhamma as a foreigner by sitting meditation (I only thought of meditating at a monastery at that time). Then I discovered one monastery associated with a Burmese *sayadaw* (monk teacher) in a province of Thailand. During a long holiday, I went alone to that monastery and tried to practice Dhamma. I had to practice alone because I considered the sayadaw was very old to coach me for my practice. I took reading materials with me to serve as daily self-discourse for motivation. There I read "The Art of Living" chapter by chapter each day of my practice. I had had that book for nearly a year and frankly I did not like it as the approach seemed too scientific. I was doing meditation as my religious achievement and I considered myself as a very obedient follower of Buddha.

But actually this book inspired me a lot and I wanted to do the course as suggested. Fortunately, I found out that Thailand had a Vipassana center near Bangkok. I registered my name for the course held in early October 1995. It was the only two weeks annual leave I received from my Company for the whole working year. This is where I came to know Vipassana in this tradition.

My older brother had taken up the practice a year earlier. I was the owner of a business, and he saw that I had a great deal of stress in my life, and so he was suggesting that I might get great benefit from going and sitting a meditation course. I had plans to go sit on a beach somewhere in the Caribbean and that was my dream. I'd been working two years continuously, had taken hardly a day off and was very desperate to have a vacation. So when he suggested meditation I thought no, I need something like just relaxing on a beach. But what he said kept sticking in my head, that from a vacation going to some place like a beach, I might get a couple of weeks of rest; by learning to meditate, I might get something that would be useful to me day in and day out. And I knew what a stressful situation I was in, so I finally gave up the idea of going on vacation and took a plane and flew to this meditation camp.

—*David Crutcher sat his first course in 1982 at the San Francisco Boy's Club Camp, USA.*

A gong rings for food. There's a tasty soup, some homemade bread or cookies and tea. Over the meal introductions are made and acquaintances struck up. For some this is their first encounter with meditation of any kind, for others it's the first taste of Vipassana in this tradition. And then there are the "old students" who have taken courses before and are coming back for more. Looking around at the mix of faces, it's a real cross-section of race, age and type. What are they hoping to get out of the course?

🍂

To be more calm within myself, make some decisions about my life and where it's going . . . .

To have less fear—and anger—to be able to confront that, look at it and work my way through it . . . .

To make a better person of myself, mentally, physically, spiritually. I'm here now, gotta do it, no turning back . . . .

. . . a way of getting in touch with my essence . . . .

. . . a learning process . . . .

. . . a new experience . . . .

—*Excerpts from interviews with first-time students, Australia 1990.*

A precourse talk follows the meal. This is done so that students are thoroughly briefed about the discipline, timetable and practicalities of living at the center during the course and have the opportunity to raise any queries. The staff and course management introduce themselves and welcome everyone to the center. The code of discipline, it is explained, exists solely to help the students get the best results from their meditation and should be followed carefully.

The first and most basic rule is that they remain for the whole course. The technique is taught step by step and ten days is the minimum period in which it is possible to learn it. If someone leaves in the middle of the course they won't give themselves a chance to learn the entire technique and they won't give the technique a chance to work for them. Therefore every individual should make a firm decision that he or she will stay for the entire period of the course, from the beginning to the end.

Noble silence is a must if someone is to get maximum advantage of the retreat. In practice this means that during the first nine days of the course, students are requested not to have any contact with fellow meditators by speech, writing or gestures. They must cut off all contact with each other, as well as with the outside world. Taking notes or writing journals is also not permitted. If there are any material problems, for instance, in relation to food, accommodation or health, students can speak with the course manager. If they have any problem or questions about the meditation, they can see the assistant teachers. Notices are posted regularly concerning the day's schedule and other points of information about the course.

On the last full day of the course students will be able to share their experiences, they'll be able to talk with each other and get reacquainted. However, during the period of serious intensive work, it's vital to maintain complete silence in order not to disturb oneself or others. Noble silence ends on the morning of day ten but the course doesn't finish until about 7:30 the following morning. This interval between the end of the intensive meditation period and reentry to regular life is an essential transition. The teaching, how to integrate the practice into daily life, continues. The last day is important and everyone is expected to stay until the very end of the course.

During the course period, students have to discontinue all other spiritual practices that they have learned and work according to the instructions they are given. This includes all forms of prayer, worship or religious ceremony as well as other meditation techniques and healing practices. This is not to condemn any other practice or technique, but to give a proper trial to the technique of Vipassana without mixing it with anything else.

To learn, one has to be receptive, to be prepared to accept the teaching with discrimination and understanding, to accept the guidance of the teacher at least for the course period. During the ten days it's essential to work exactly according to the instructions, without adding or omitting anything. At the end of the course, the student can decide which practice best suits them.

In order to preserve the meditative atmosphere, it's important that students remain within the course boundaries and avoid contact with anyone from outside. Separate walking areas are provided for men and women. Complete segregation of the sexes will be observed throughout and there should be no physical contact between members of the same or opposite sex. Couples, friends or family members should not communicate in any way during the intensive period of the course.

Vipassana, the talk concludes, is a technique of self observation. To succeed at it, try to work as if you are alone, working in isolation, keeping to yourself. Try not to create distractions for others and ignore any distractions that might occur. The course will begin shortly. We wish you all success.

After a few final questions the meeting ends and everyone prepares for the first sitting in the meditation

hall. Even before the course begins, the discipline of silence takes effect. A stillness in the dusk. As they wait,
students alone with their thoughts at the beginning of a
journey inside.

I hung the brochure with the course schedule on the wall
of my room, and often looked at it in disbelief. Counting
the meditation periods, I kept thinking, is that really ten
hours? Are they nuts? Am I nuts? What am I doing here?
Why am I doing this to myself? Something had drawn
me to the place, certainly, but as the ten-day course geared
up to begin, I still could not pinpoint what it was.

It had taken an encounter with an old student, a Western
manager of an Indian center, to shift my Vipassana pot
from the back to the front burner. I remember this man
with much gratitude. He was about my age, an American
and WASPy, like myself, so there was that ingress from
the start. But what sold me on the course was his lack of
salesmanship, and the intangible something that he
radiated when he spoke of Vipassana and Dhamma. He
was just what I needed, at just the right time. Instead of
pontificating or preaching, I remember him quietly
smiling at my questions and saying, "If you are attracted,
then just go sit."

> —*Marty Cooper is studying counselling psychology*
> *at a graduate school in San Francisco. He is also*
> *a drummer, writer and political activist.*

All was so sudden. I had been so much in love and we
recently split and it was so painful, so painful. And,
suddenly, I decided that it was enough. Enough suffering.
All of a sudden I chose the non-desire stream. I went
from desire to non-desire. It was very clear. No pain
anymore. And within a few weeks I found myself sitting
a ten-day Vipassana course directed by S.N. Goenka at
Bodh Gaya in India, the place where Buddha became
enlightened. That was in February 1977. Before that I

had practiced meditation for twenty years but I never sat an intensive period. Always one hour at the most.

So, when my younger daughter (who was around 17) decided she would not see me any more, I naturally thought: "Am I so bad that both my girlfriend and my daughter don't want to see me again?" And I began to search for a long period of meditation, some intensive program which could change me.

—Jean-Claude See was a painter and film maker before training and practicing as a psychotherapist. Retired now, he lives in Paris, France.

Had a girl say to me, "When you came up here, you were so drawn and so lined . . ." Was I, I thought? I didn't know.

—Excerpt from precourse interview with first-time student, Australia 1990

By the age of 25 when I began meditating, I had already gone through challenging times of life where I was involved with recreational drugs such as marijuana, hashish, cocaine, and hallucinogenic drugs. I had been caught by the police once for possession of drugs when I was 16 years old, which was reported to my parents. I also went through a time of stealing things from shops, other people and generally feeling like I could take anything that was around! I was caught three different times by shops and my parents were informed. Perhaps surprisingly, my upbringing was very comfortable financially and emotionally. I was brought up in the city; my father worked successfully as a professional. My parents were committed to each other and to parenting. And I was given every educational, social, and sporting opportunity I could imagine—private schools, ski houses, summer houses on the beach, after school programs in sports and arts. My last big ignorance was sequential sexual relationships; this proved the hardest pattern to break, even after I began meditating.

—Jenni Parker, Chicago, USA

I was on my way to my ninth meditation retreat and I admit to having felt heavily jaded. I was attending with a been-there-done-that attitude. My first retreat had been in India thirty-one years before. I'd wanted to become a monk, to give away all my worldly belongings at 21 and become a student of the Dhamma, on my way to a quick and romantic enlightenment. Like many young acolytes, I soon found the path to be steeper than I had bargained for and stepped rather quickly back into my comfortable householder slippers. But the habit of regular meditation had stuck, along with a pattern of suffering the occasional ten-day "tune up," so highly recommended by Gotama the Buddha as the true path of ultimate liberation . . . .

I arrived at Bragg Creek camp (Alberta) where the course had been organized knowing full well that the basement of my heart was choked with the junk of decades, that my two hour daily meditation practice hadn't even begun to clear away the weighty debris. I knew that I was barely "maintaining," that I needed help of some sort that I hadn't been getting. I'd done three types of group therapy, four meditation courses, and seen one therapist within the past couple of years. Good stuff, perhaps, but it all failed to get to the root of my problems. It was clear that I needed something else.

I had heard about the intensity of the course schedule in this tradition of Vipassana; the emphasis for eleven hours a day on sitting meditation. So I was apprehensive going into the ten-day commitment, but I also welcomed the challenge. I knew that there would be a fair bit of "*tapas*" (fire, friction) generated and that was exactly what I needed before I would start to feel any clearer and lighter.

After checking in and being shown to my room in the summer camp dorm, I felt some mild letdown. "Oh . . .

this again," said my mind. "We've done this before and . . . here we are again. What, exactly, is the point?"

I really wasn't sure.

—Jason Farrell, a teacher and writer, lives in Canada.

❧

I had always felt, from the time I was a teenager, that I was going to find some practice, something very different and very ancient that would have great meaning in my life. So, I had tried . . . I'd read numerous books and I had had some experiences with various other kinds of technique, but none of them I'd ever taken up with any kind of depth.

So when I came to this camp where the course was being held, I started out with fear of the fact that this might be some kind of brainwashing technique. As I was on the plane this came up for me, but I entered the course because of confidence in my brother, for whom I have a great respect.

—David Crutcher, USA

Chapter 4

THE COURSE EXPERIENCE—DURING

The busy course program is designed to help the students, newcomers and those with previous experience, get the very most from their retreat. The teaching is presented systematically through daily instructions and talks. Students have the opportunity to meditate by themselves and as a group; their progress is periodically checked by the conducting teachers. Although meditators are asked to maintain silence among themselves for the first nine days of the course, support and help is always at hand from the teachers and course managers.

The day begins at 4:30 a.m. with students meditating in their rooms or in the hall, where a chanting tape is played. Breakfast is at 6:30, followed by a group sitting in the hall and instructions. Individual meditation then continues and the teachers meet and meditate with students in small groups. Old students may be allocated their own meditation rooms or cells to enable them to work more independently and seriously. Lunch comes at 11:00; simple, nutritious, vegetarian food is served. A two-hour break in the middle of the day gives everyone a chance to rest, do their washing or exercise outside. The teachers are available for individual student interviews at this time. Meditation and checking continue in the afternoon. Tea and fruit for new students and lemon water or juice for old students are served at 5:00. After the final session of group meditation, a taped evening discourse by S.N. Goenka clarifies each day's practice. The teachers are again available after the talk to answer questions and students retire to bed by 9:30.

To learn Vipassana there are three steps to the training: morality, mastery of mind and the development of insight. The course opens with some important formalities and initial instructions. The commitment to follow a simple moral code forms the foundation for successful meditation practice. By making deliberate efforts not to kill, or lie, or steal; not to engage in sexual misconduct, or take intoxicants, one contributes to the well-being of the community. But equally one is acting in one's own self interest. As one develops in meditation it becomes clear that to perform any unwholesome action at the physical or vocal level, one must first generate intense negativity in the mind. Only then will misdeeds result. By living a moral life, we prevent our minds from becoming tainted in ways that will be self-evidently harmful to ourselves and our neighbors. We also pave the way for effective meditation by freeing the mind of agitation, keeping it calm and quiet.

The Buddha repeatedly emphasized the preeminence of mind over physical and vocal actions and the practical consequences of our mental attitude. In contrasting verses, he explains:

> *If you speak or act with an impure mind,*
> *suffering follows, just as the wheel follows*
> *the ox pulling the cart;*
> *If you speak or act with a pure mind,*
> *happiness follows like a shadow*
> *that never leaves.*

—Dhammapada, 1,2

The law of cause and effect (Pāli: *kamma*) always operates, he reminds us, whether we are aware of it or not, whether we like it or not. Payback is a fact. Inevitably we do reap as we sow.

To begin to meditate, we need something on which to focus our attention. There are many different techniques of meditation, using various methods to concentrate the mind—a word or phrase; an image; an object; contemplating one's thoughts. However Vipassana, without condemning them, avoids all these approaches for one very significant reason. The goal of the technique is nothing less than total purification of the mind, for which concentration is a means, not an end in itself. The most suitable preparation for the practice of Vipassana is the exercise of developing awareness of respiration (Pāli: ānāpāna). This is the practice the students begin that first evening of the course and will develop over the next three and a half days.

The student sits in a comfortable position with back and neck straight. Eyes and mouth are gently closed. One fixes one's full attention at the entrance of the nostrils, just observing the breath as it passes in and out. If the awareness is not distinct, one can intentionally breathe slightly hard for a few minutes before returning to the normal, natural breath, the reality of the moment, which is the object of attention.

The exercise itself is simple. Young children can understand and do it. In addition, it is completely nonsectarian and acceptable to all. And yet, the practice is not easy. Why? As soon as we try to be aware of respiration, a revolt begins in mind and body. Our system is not used to this discipline and aches and pains break out all over. At the same time, we are irritated to find that the mind finds a thousand distractions and seems quite unable to carry out this elementary task. Yet by persevering with the practice, we start to realize through our own inner experience certain important truths about the mind. Even though it is not the direct object of meditation, we begin to see how cluttered with thoughts and feelings the mind is; how wild and lacking in order; how it prefers to roll in memories of the past or speculation about the future rather than being in the present; how, if not lost in fantasies, it rolls in greed and hatred. It requires all our patience and persistence to keep proceeding in the face of a barrage of internal difficulties. With experience we come to accept how dull and crude the mind can be and smile at it. The difficulties too are part of the process; we learn not to become dejected or disillusioned when concentration seems impossible. Our job is just to keep trying. The simple act of maintaining proper efforts carries us through, and little by little the storms die down and awareness does indeed become established.

With continuous practice, the awareness becomes sharper and we are able to feel subtler objects in the area of mouth and nostrils, the touch of the breath, the temperature of the breath and even sensations which have no connection with the respiration. The mind meanwhile becomes more tame and amenable, allowing us to concentrate for longer periods without interruption. By observing the natural sensations in one limited area of the body and learning not to react to them, we are ready to begin the real work of purification: Vipassana.

There was a lot of resistance in my mind, though it had received such gentle and patient preparation. Experimentation with aids to sitting comfortably had been endless and the result was perfect. Little physical discomfort was experienced as I tried to attend exclusively to the practice of Anapana, and silence and half-light in the meditation hall was especially helpful. Sometimes, the small area of floor space it was possible to allocate to each student, was proving to be a big problem. But then, so too, was aloneness and boredom in my room at night, particularly during wakeful periods, which were many. Perhaps boredom and non-activity were syndromes least well tolerated. They are states rarely experienced in daylight waking hours, so I fretted quite severely and resented the repetition of my attention's direction on to

watching and returning to the small areas on my upper
lip. Nothing much appeared to be happening there, but I
discovered the abysmal lack of concentration and patience
I had! My mind's restless and wayward habit was revealed
to me for the first time. I was shocked, and found even
very short episodes of stillness rare.

The concept "Be here now" has always attracted me. I
was learning a little how to experience it for the first time
ever. Much agitation and aversion arose in me as the days
followed one another; and such strong negative urges!
To escape was one, often repeated in my mind. However,
instructions and much assistance, clear and strong, upheld
my wavering resolution.

—Jessie Brown, age 80, caregiver and housewife,
lives in Gloucestershire, UK and has been
meditating for over twenty years.

The first day of sitting cross-legged was agony. I am fifty
years old and have an old back injury which became
extremely painful and my knees and ankles also hurt. I
had made a commitment to stay for ten days and I have
always believed in keeping to my commitments. However
I could not imagine that I could bear ten times as much
pain and it seemed that there was no hope for completing
the course. I approached the assistant teacher with my
problem and he suggested sitting with my back to the
wall. This was immediately before Goenkaji's first video
discourse, and I was enthralled by what he had to say. He
described my experience and his style was so refreshing
to me that my spirits lifted. Never before had I
encountered such wisdom that was consistent with my
own experience. I looked forward to future discourses.

As the days went by the pain didn't get any better, but
then about the third day I was thinking, "My leg is in
pain," and suddenly the meaning of the words and the
experience coincided—my legs were in pain but I was not,
I was an observer of my legs in pain. I recognized that
this was a technique that I had used at the dentist to avoid

panic and pain and from then on I was mostly able to
observe the pain without becoming involved in the cyclical
chain of avoidance. I enjoyed Goenkaji's second and third
discourses also and was struck by the description of the
mind as being full of chattering monkeys and wild horses
with the odd rampaging elephant. I know that this is a
true description for all people, but I'd been considered
by my friends to have an additional dose and to use
thinking to excess. It was a real battle to get control of
my mind but I was hooked on the idea and very
determined.

> —*Ron Thompson gave up a computer software ca-*
> *reer to become a philosopher. He sat his first*
> *Vipassana retreat at Kaukapakapa,*
> *New Zealand in 1998.*

On the second day of his first Vipassana course S.N.
Goenka nearly ran away. In Rangoon at his teacher's center, meditators were allowed to talk during the first days of
the course—the period of Anapana. Naturally they discussed their different experiences of meditation. On the
second day fellow students recounted to him their experiences of "divine sight" and "divine sound." According to
his preconceived notions of meditation, these were signs
of high attainment, far superior to the observation of ordinary breath and sensations which he had been diligently
practicing.

All afternoon I was full of dejection. An overpowering
conviction arose in me that, as was said by a saintly person,
it is easier for a camel to pass through the eye of a needle
than for a rich man to enter the gates of the kingdom of
heaven. Here was I, a rich man, looking for entry into
the kingdom of heaven—an impossible job. No wonder
these other meditators were more successful than I—they
were quiet people without the twisted mind of a
businessman, not involved in the rat race of making
money.

By evening, I had made up my mind to give up the course and to go back home. Every day at 5:00 p.m., a car came from my house with fresh laundry and other necessities. I was sure that the Teacher would not give his consent to my leaving, I decided to slip away in my car that evening.

Goenka went to his room and began to pack. Fortunately however a fellow meditator sensed he was in difficulties and went to speak with him. When he explained why he was leaving, she urged him to forget about this craving for divine lights or sounds. The Teacher was pleased with his progress, why not try for just one more day?

Inspired by her words, Goenka once again settled down to meditate, determined to give all importance to respiration and sensation in the nostrils and mouth area and to forget about anything else, as his teacher had asked him to do. Very soon, as his mind became concentrated, he experienced a bright starlike light and soon after other extrasensory experiences began to occur. These were what he had been craving; but now he understood that his task was to observe the objects of meditation only and to ignore any distractions. The timely intervention of this kindly lady stopped him from running away and missing something of priceless value to a human being.

At the start of the course I experienced little more than resentment and disorientation. Everything was wrong, wrong, wrong: the technique, so different to what I was used to; my place in the hall among the new students despite years of sitting; the teachers. But I had agreed to give everything I had to the technique and within a day or two I started to notice some subtle but very interesting changes—a breaking up of the density that had been my "normal" experience.

Leaving the meditation hall on the third morning, I encountered an orange tabby cat. She looked at me while

I was slipping into my sandals and I saw that she was missing her right eye, just like me. My instant reaction was that this made her special, not lame or in any way deficient as I had always semiconsciously considered myself to be as a result of my disfiguring accident at age three. My immediate acceptance of the cat transferred to myself instantaneously and I burst into tears. Wow! Pure self-acceptance! What a wonderfully unlooked-for joy!

This was my first experience of a crack in my thick and well-kept armor that allowed a little exultation to seep through. It was such a relief to be able to think of myself or to feel myself as whole, as being perfectly and gloriously who I am, weird-looking blind eye and all . . . .

—*Jason Farrell, Canada*

The discipline was quite strict but personally I think it needed to be. For me, I needed a kick. There's this battle going on—part of me saying "This is great. I want to go to India to do a thirty-day retreat"; and the other part saying "Are you crazy? What are you doing here? This is hard, you must be out of your mind!" I knew there'd be a battle before I came here, but the longer I stayed I learned to observe that—"okay I'm going through this thing; let's just watch it."

—*Excerpt from postcourse interview with first-time student, Australia 1990*

The center was very nice, peaceful, with a lot of trees, bushes and plants between the dormitories. I shared my room with a Canadian who on three occasions during the ten days was so deep in his meditations that he accidentally locked me in the room by bolting the door from the outside. This placed me in a dilemma—should I break noble silence by shouting for help or should I risk missing the group sittings? (I ended up rattling the door until someone took pity on me.)

—*Tony White, UK*

The teaching of Vipassana is given on the fourth day of the course. By this time the students have settled into the silent rhythm of the program. With the help of the breath, they've had some success in focusing and calming the wayward mind. Their understanding of the practice too is growing through their own direct experience of the meditation, the explanations and encouragement in the discourses and regular interaction with the conducting teachers.

The object of meditation in Vipassana is once again universal and completely nonsectarian. With the heightened awareness accomplished during Anapana, one moves the attention throughout the entire body, from head to feet and feet to head, scanning every part of the body and introspecting each and every sensation one observes on the way.

Along with this expansion in the area of awareness, comes another complementary aspect of the technique—developing equanimity, the ability to keep a balanced mind whatever the nature of the sensations one meets.

The sensations on the body, real normal physical sensations—like heat, heaviness, perspiration, pain, numbness, tingling, vibrating—are at the core of the meditation practice taught by the Buddha.

*Everything in the mind flows along with sensations
on the body.*
                              —Mūlaka Sutta; Aṅguttara Nikāya

In this single sentence he pinpoints the interrelationship between mind and body. If our thoughts really do manifest with physical sensations, then ultimately we can learn to "read" our minds with the help of our bodies. But more immediately, by learning not to react to the sensations, whether they are pleasant, unpleasant or neutral, we stop creating tensions for ourselves now and allow past mental conditioning to surface and unravel. This was the authentic path of purification the Buddha discovered, beyond the extremes of austerity and license, which took him to full enlightenment—a state of indescribable happiness where all mental impurities have been eradicated.

At first, as we survey the body in meditation, we tend to encounter mostly solidified, coarse-type sensations; or else blank areas where there appear to be no sensations at all. By working calmly however, we find that, if we can manage not to react to these unpleasant sensations, their intensity naturally dissolves. We begin to experience for ourselves the arising and passing away of sensations on the body—sometimes slowly, sometimes with great rapidity—ultimately reaching a stage where we feel no solidity in the body whatsoever.

With growing objectivity, we are able to appreciate the interrelationship between body and mind, and the impermanent nature of both. At the mental level, thoughts and emotions keep surging up during meditation. Following the technique, we learn neither to express this flow of mental content, such as anger, passion, fear and sadness, nor to suppress it. Rather, we practice to simply observe the sensations or the breathing which arise along with the mental content. The more successful we are in the practice, the more bare observation and understanding cancel out and replace the tendencies to greed, hatred and ignorance in our minds.

Through practicing Vipassana we begin to explore for ourselves the Four Noble Truths which the Buddha taught. First, the truth of suffering, so clear both physically and mentally when we sit in meditation, and made "noble" in precious moments of wisdom when we can just observe and not react. And what causes this suffering but constant craving and attachment to our selves and our desires? Realizing this cause experientially is the second truth. "I" has

become so important and letting go, whether it be possessions, opinions or surrendering to our own inevitable end,
has become so hard. This is one half of the picture. But the
teaching is optimistic as well as realistic. Insight developed
through meditation also reveals to us the third truth—that
there is another way: we do have a choice to reduce and
finally eliminate our suffering. Not only is there really an
end to adversity, which we experience working with sensations in our practice, but this path—the fourth noble truth:
living a moral life, controlling and purifying the mind—is
taking us towards that high goal.

Having so often noted the laws of nature in the outside world: in the flux of the tides; night and day; birth,
life and death; we now begin to realize how these same
laws apply inside each one of us. We begin to see and accept that this continuous state of change which we are
witnessing is entirely impersonal and operating beyond our
control, despite constant attempts on our part to identify
with it. The truth breaks over us like a rising dawn that
everything we experience is essentially unsatisfactory in
character—either because it is not to our liking or, if we do
desire it, because it too will pass away soon enough.
Vipassana gives us the capacity to be fully aware of everything that is taking place—breaching the barrier between
conscious and unconscious mind. Vipassana also helps to
train the mind to remain detached in every situation, moving beyond the push and pull of sensations, towards real
peace.

Today anyone can practice this technique, and with
proper guidance and sincere efforts, they can take steps
towards the same ultimate goal. Meditator or no, we may
feel intuitively that this account of the mind-body phenomenon is correct, yet it takes time to understand the
process for ourselves. Continuous change, suffering and
egolessness (Pāli: *anicca, dukkha* and *anattā*) characterize
our worldly existence. A teacher can only show the way,

the Buddha said. He or she cannot liberate anyone. Each individual has to make one's own bid for freedom.

One day after another the students on the course work more seriously. Practicing Vipassana clears space for deep personal change, therefore old habits facing eviction put up a fight. Obstacles to their meditation keep surfacing: intense likes and dislikes, drowsiness, agitation, waves of doubt. Students are relieved to learn this is quite normal. With determination and courage they are increasingly able to stand their ground and ride out the storms. They are growing in confidence. There's a deepening appreciation of the teaching and the strength of mind they are achieving.

In meditation the science of mind and body reveals itself to us. We examine ourselves both at the physical and mental level with the aid of body feelings. There is no reliance on God or divine forces to attain the result. We take upon ourselves the responsibility for the reality of the present. The future will then take care of itself, while the hold the past has over us gradually weakens.

Through the practice of Vipassana meditation we begin to see what actually is taking place in mind and body moment to moment. For instance, an unpleasant incident occurs, an argument with a friend or the car won't start, and I react angrily—in response, it seems, to this external situation. However, investigating the truth at the depth of the mind, the Buddha discovered a missing link between stimulus and response. Some sensation or other arises in the body as a result of the initial experience and it is to this sensation that we react, not in fact to the outside world. A biochemical flow is constantly being triggered and released inside which manifests as different sensations.

Previously we were either unaware of this subtle mind-body phenomenon or we were continually overwhelmed by these body sensations and our reactions to them. A habit pattern full of blocks, obsessions, confusions, fantasies and complexes was created, with no-one but ourselves to blame. This resulted in entrenched views and behaviors, without any apparent relief or release. And because nothing in the world, inside or outside ourselves, remains fixed, a constant process of multiplication of accumulated impurity (Pāli: *saṅkhāra*) was piling up misery upon misery for us. Little wonder, at times, that without a technique to provide perspective and direction, someone despairs at their ability to shift this burden. But with Vipassana, there is a way out. By training our minds to observe sensations without reaction, we can halt the negative process in which we have become trapped. Not only do we gain immediate benefit from avoiding blind reactions, we also begin to clear out the impurities deep inside—the reverse process, a virtuous cycle, has been set in motion. The insight we develop helps us find skilful solutions to our problems.

If the body is not given food, it will eventually die. However, despite starvation, it is able to continue for several weeks—why? Because the fats and other materials within the physical structure are sufficient to sustain it for a limited period. The mind, which constantly requires some kind of input, works in a similar way. If we stop generating and ingesting negative thoughts and emotions, the stock of impurity made in the past gets released. By facing the problem, we are relieved of it.

Rechargeable batteries work on the same principle. To discharge you need do nothing—just stop the current from coming in. Anyone is welcome to try for themselves and see the truth of this. The wisdom of others, in written and spoken form, we can only receive secondhand and never possess. We can use the intellect for critical thinking but it will not solve the fundamental problems of existence, which lie beyond its reach. If, however, inspiration and reasoning lead us to develop our own wise understanding through personal experience, they will have served a worthwhile purpose; for this personal wisdom alone will liberate the mind

and convince us that the technique works. The Buddha himself recommended this pragmatic approach to adopting a
spiritual path—not to be swayed by a teacher, a tradition,
speculation or the view of the majority:

> *... after observation and analysis, when it agrees*
> *with reason and is conducive to the good and gain of*
> *one and all, then accept it and live up to it.*
>
> —Kālāma Sutta, Aṅguttara Nikāya

Sitting a ten-day course, we can give our undivided attention to this introspective process. Working to an
intensive schedule and making continuous efforts, we can
indeed train the mind to the task of self observation. Not
that we will become perfect by the end of a single course,
but we gain an outline of the technique and the experience
of the sensations in relation to mind and body. We feel the
changes taking place inside, we gain the tools to carry us
through life and soon we will have the chance to put the
practice to use.

❦

When Goenkaji explained the Four Noble Truths on that
first night, I embraced the First Noble Truth with
acceptance and relief. There I was, on my honeymoon,
living out dreams I had had for years and yet I was
painfully unhappy with my husband, myself and my life.
I finally had to face the truth for myself that life is indeed
suffering.

With the first Anapana instructions, I felt elated. For a
few years, I had been intrigued with the idea of observing
breath but hadn't known how to go about it. Suddenly
here was the way to do it, and with such a clear purpose:
to concentrate the mind! As the course progressed, I
struggled with my agitated mind and extreme pain all over
my body. By the time Vipassana instructions were given,
the pain was beginning to feel overwhelming. As we
moved our awareness through the body to observe the

sensations, trying not to react, I understood and fully accepted that this is the way to come out of suffering. I realized that I had finally found what I had been looking for in my life even though I hadn't known it.

—*Karen Donovan, USA*

A medical doctor was specializing in abnormal and clinical psychology when he and a friend took their first retreat.
My mind was never accepting of blind faith. I participated in the Vipassana course with doubt nurtured by direct experience of prevalent spiritual hypocrisy. However this doubt was tempered with scientific openness. A strange event took place there. Doubt evaporated and real faith sprouted. A scientific mind bowed down in reverence. The experiment was conducted for ten days in strictly controlled conditions. I tried to work with full sincerity. The vow of silence was strictly observed. Instructions were literally followed.

Unaccustomed to sit in one posture for a long time, my mind was very much agitated for the initial two to three days. But that initial agitation had to surrender to strong determination. With the very start of Vipassana impurity exploded in the eyes which turned red and sore, continuously emitting thick discharge for several days. Aware that eruptions of impurities can happen during the practice, this did not cause discouragement or any obstruction. Due to eye soreness, my eyes were mostly kept closed or downcast which was helpful to meditation. Before joining the course I had been passing through a very critical and stressful period of life for the previous couple of years. Now clouds of stress and strain evaporated and the mind-system was thoroughly cleansed, becoming full of freshness, liveliness and lightness. Gradually the eye trouble subsided and after two or three days at the end of the course it was all right.

—*Dr Ram Nayan Singh, Postgraduate College,*
Ghazipur, India

When we had become adjusted to detecting the subtle body sensations I was immediately able to observe old and present injuries and some improvement was noticed. I soon became aware of sensations in my lower abdomen which relate to some discomfort in my bowels. Observing these sensations relieves the discomfort.

At times I became very clear of gross sensations and was able to sweep my entire body from head to feet and back several times per second. At such times the individual sensations from every part of my body were quite clear and very precisely located so that it seemed like my awareness was very many times greater in a very much smaller time. At other times gross sensations dominated parts of my body and sweeping was impossible. I fell into the trap of craving and aversion for these conditions and gave myself a roller coaster ride being at incredible highs with the most magic energy coursing through me and then within a day being in the depths of despair.

—Ron Thompson, New Zealand

I found it a strange combination of torture and tranquillity. The sitting position was so uncomfortable it felt to me that all my joints would dislocate. My mind wouldn't stay on the simple subject of observing my sensations. It seemed to find remembering sexual encounters far more interesting. This I found totally infuriating. But, gradually as the days progressed into an enjoyable routine, I felt a tranquillity that I knew I had been searching for for years. By the time the course ended (all too soon), I felt that I was just getting the hang of it.

—Tony White, UK

On the fifth or sixth day of the course, my awareness of sensations penetrated inside the body. The teacher was very kind to interview me every day and solved my difficulties through these discussions. On the sixth night I could barely get to sleep and the next day when I met him my teacher said "Thanda, you always say "I had to, I had to," a lot. Do you think you are the one doing all things yourself?"

I answered, "Sir, I still think the mind is my mind and my mind is making everything happen."

He replied "To practice Dhamma effort should be at minimum. Try reducing the effort you put in."

From that time on, I tried to observe my way of meditation—putting too much effort into working, too much I will do, I am doing (BIG I). I saw I was identifying with the sensations. Finally, sitting with "no effort," I realized that sensations come naturally and go naturally. They come and go not because I am doing something but because of their nature. At the same time I could see myself, how proud, how self-centered, how selfish, I was. These experiences were things I will not forget for my whole life.

—*Thanda Win, Myanmar*

It was a real struggle—full of ups and downs and but I knew it had to be good because it was so simple, pure and most of all about practice, practice, practice. Like the bitterest and most natural remedies, it proved to be the most beneficial, the sweetest in its reward. The course was highlighted by many Dhamma brothers and sisters working hard, incredible teatime sunset watchings, beautiful night sits punctuated by the chirping and croaking of one solitary frog, skies full of shining stars and galaxies, the howls of coyotes mournfully crying out their existence, a spider's web full with early morning dew hanging perfection, a ghost face halo on nearby plants.

On occasions, time seemed very different—distinct, sharper, the edges of all things glowing with *anicca*, the impermanence of all things. As I looked from clock, to tea steam, to crimson sunset, to quivering grass, to

chalkmark jet streams in the opaque blue sky, I realized
anicca as a truth.

> —*Max Kiely, a 26 year old Canadian elementary*
> *schoolteacher, artist and healer,*
> *first found Vipassana at Dhamma*
> *Mahāvana, California in 1997.*

The meditation practice wasn't so deep because of baby's
pushings. He didn't want me to sit in the hall for more
than ten minutes at a time. And the best words for him
were "May all beings be happy!" when he moved strongly
and then relaxed at last.

> —*Olga Mamykina, a physician, took a course at a*
> *nearby rented site towards the end of her*
> *first pregnancy. She lives with her husband*
> *and young son in Moscow, Russia.*

It's quite informative to look back and compare the quality
of successive mornings, especially the early 4:30 to 6:30
session when I was experiencing the most difficulty. On
the first day I was wholly the resenter. I had a very difficult
time handling my noisy fellow meditators, my recorded
teacher and my enforced and seemingly superficial new
meditation technique. By the fifth morning, what other
people were doing simply didn't matter; I had too much
going on inside to give noises and judgments any energy.
And by the eighth morning I was more than capable of
beaming loving acceptance to all my brothers and sisters,
the brave and gallant souls who had chosen to plumb the
depths of their own inner waters for all these tempestuous
days. My heart was absolutely open to all of them and no
resentment was possible or even conceivable . . . .

Coming to the course, my task had been to clean up
the cluttered basement of my mind. I had begun it with a
great weight of drudgery attached like a ball-and-chain
to the job but there I was on day eight in the same
basement and with much of the same garbage cluttering

it up and I was feeling pretty good about it. The sole difference was my attitude. I had come to recognize on a very deep level that I could love my own silly garbage! I didn't even have to chuck it all out immediately and discovered that it was lots easier to laugh about it than agonize over what to do with it.

—*Jason Farrell, Canada*

🐚

The first steps are always the hardest in anything you want to do, but once you make that step . . . Like I do a lot of work in gold mining, dredging, the first ounce is the hardest to get, but once you get it, you're away . . . .

—*Excerpt from postcourse interview with first-time student, Australia 1990.*

On the morning of the tenth day, a new type of practice is taught: the meditation of loving kindness (Pāli: *mettā bhāvanā*). This final part of Vipassana has a different focus and uses an altogether different technique. For Vipassana it is essential to maintain one's attention on the sensations within the framework of the body, to carry out the work of self-purification. However, to practice Metta, the sharing of all one has gained with others, one deliberately fills these same sensations with feelings of goodwill and compassion, which radiate throughout the body and into the atmosphere beyond. Having first worked to purify oneself, sending vibrations of harmony and selfless love to others is an integral part of the meditation practice, producing powerful positive effects.

From now on, as they approach the end of the course and prepare to reconnect with the world outside, the meditators will practice a few minutes of Metta after every sitting of Vipassana.

🐚

Later I again began to feel awash in the ecstatic feeling. Instead of pulsing through, the feeling persisted in my body, in fact it seemed to be what my body was made of. The immediate environment seemed essentially identical. Into this environment I felt the arrival of my parents. They had died about six months apart approximately ten years earlier. Now they were back with me in a realistic and very powerful way. I loved them in a whole and healing manner. I felt that everything in our past together was just as it should have been and that everything was complete. This brought a sense of final closure with any dissatisfaction I had ever had and a new flow of love for them.

By now the feeling of love and the sensation of ecstasy had become intertwined. They seemed to be as one. And then another new aspect of this ecstasy began to assert itself. Before this I had seemed to be the passive recipient. Now I came to feel that I produced it from somewhere within me. I flooded my parents with it and then began to produce it in ever greater quantity until it began to flow upward out of me. This flow went straight upward until it encountered a substantial blanket of similar material which encapsulated the whole globe. That which I produced turned rather abruptly when it encountered the blanket and flowed along within it, fully integrated, yet maintaining its distinct identity. It flowed laterally toward some unknown destination and then it turned abruptly downward. Its destination was my ex-wife and my brother, both located in Seattle. These were the two living people with whom love and problems created a strong response in my life. Now I was pouring love into them. As with my parents, there was now only love in great abundance.

Ultimately, the strongest part of the experience was not with any of the four people it involved, but rather with the thick blanket of love which I felt to be encompassing the earth.

—*Charles Brown, USA*

People sometimes feel that meditation is an introverted and rather selfish activity. "What about the ills of the world while you are contemplating your navel!" Vipassana *is* a self centered technique in the sense that only by working correctly on ourselves can we really be in a position to help others. But the whole thrust of the meditation is towards dissolving the false ego we have created and which now controls us. Little by little, as we transcend selfish egotism, we naturally want to turn the inner-directed energy and insight outwards. In this way we complete the circle of self and others.

Learning Vipassana meditation is a lifetime job. We continue to work with the same simple technique as we progress on the path, expanding and deepening our sensitivity and balance of mind. A range of practical tools is being acquired and internalized to apply whenever and wherever it may be required. We own that pile of dirty washing, it's a fact, but for anyone established in the practice there's no doubting the ability of this soap to bring it all up clean and bright.

Noble silence is lifted after the teaching of Metta. As they emerge from the meditation hall, students greet each other warmly like long-lost friends. At last they can exchange experiences and review where they stand.

So how was the silence?

Hard for a few days, feeling conditioned somehow to communicate like over breakfast. From then on it was fine, blissful even.

Bit of a problem getting the voice going again!

—excerpts from post-course interviews with
first-time students, Australia 1990

The intensive phase of the course is done. Now is the time to become extroverted again while still maintaining contact with the truth inside, the time to see how to integrate Vipassana with everyday living. Group sittings and discourses continue until the following morning but the program for the final day is deliberately lighter and more flexible to help along the process of adjustment.

There is laughter and ease over lunch as the stories flow.

Although the course was tough, it wasn't all seriousness—after all, we're dealing with human beings. There were some hilarious moments. Like the meditator to my left who was an old gentleman and had been permitted, in view of his condition, to use a chair. The sweet old man would usually come a little late for the meditation sessions and then promptly fall asleep, snoring gently. In spite of his infirmity I noticed he was usually the first to get his meal. Then there was an incident on the eighth day during one of the group sittings. I felt a stinging pain on my right foot and then another and I thought "My God, ants. What am I going to do?" Then another thought entered my head: was it at all possible that my bad *saṅkhāras* were coming out in this form, in which case it was all the more important that I be equanimous. I tried to keep calm even though I suffered a few more burning sensations on my thigh. Finally the hour came to an end and I immediately examined my burning foot. You guessed it—they were ants!

—Professor P.N. Shankar is Deputy Director at the National Aerospace Laboratories in Bangalore, India. His wife, Priti, a professor at the Indian Institute of Science, also practices Vipassana.

In one of the dining rooms a visual display has been mounted of Vipassana centers around the world, with details of contacts and course schedules for the coming months. There's also an exhibition of books and taped materials about Vipassana and information about where they can be purchased. In the afternoon there will be a short talk explaining how someone (all "old students" now) can get involved in service of different kinds.

That night conversations often continue long after lights-out. Then suddenly it's morning and after one final strong sitting, the course is over.

In an hour or two some of our meditators will be back in front of the computer screen, at meetings or cuddling the baby. Others will wait a while, enjoying the peace, helping around the site, swapping addresses, before moving out.

As the days passed, I continually wondered if Tim was experiencing the same benefits and feeling the same appreciation and gratitude for the technique that I was. After Metta was taught on day ten, I quickly went to look for him and found him outside at the display board. He was examining the upcoming course schedule and found a course that we would attend three months later in Japan! We were delighted to discover that our enthusiasm and appreciation was mutual.

—*Karen Donovan, USA*

Madhu Sapre from Mumbai is twenty-six years of age. She's an arts graduate and an accomplished athlete. By chance she took up modelling when she was nineteen and it became her profession. Almost immediately she was made Miss India, then runner-up to Miss Universe—and her life changed drastically. She went to London and Paris to work and it all seemed great fun.

From '91 to '96 I didn't have time, or rather didn't take out time, even to breathe. I was just going with the flow. I was very lucky to have so many opportunities. But never once did I sit back and think "Who am I? What do I want?"

Outwardly everything was great. I was famous, looking good, making good money, travelling etc. . . . But I was breaking inside. I had two or three nervous breakdowns. I went to three or four shrinks. But nothing helped. I was going crazy. Every day my situation was becoming worse. I started taking pills to go to sleep but my mind was overworking so much that even that wouldn't help. I started to fear facing each day. If I wasn't working I would lock myself in my room and cry continuously. I could not believe that the relationship with my boyfriend, whom I loved more than my life, wasn't working. I became obsessive. I started self-pitying. I could not forget the past, the beautiful time we had together. I just couldn't see the reality for what it was—in the present. As well as insomnia, I also had eating disorders and used to starve myself for fifteen to twenty days.

Then there was the tension of work. I had to put up a face for other people. Slowly, slowly, I lost interest in everything. I started thinking of ways of killing myself. I had become so self-centered that I didn't even realize that my parents (with whom I was living) were also suffering so much.

Basically I was in a mess. I thought soon I'll be clinically mad. And then my father told me to come to Vipassana. In fact I had heard about the technique about three years back from my ad agency owner in London. She had attended a few courses herself. But at that time I took it very lightly. Then when my father mentioned it to me, I remembered Josie and decided to come on a course myself.

Actually when I arrived here I only knew that you are not supposed to talk, that's all.

I had no idea about the meditation program and that this was going to change my life . . . .

When we got Vipassana on the fourth day I felt I was going mad. I didn't know what was going on in my body. I just went to my room and started howling. Because there was so much pain and sensations. I was ready to go home. I said to myself I can't deal with this.

But also I was very much disturbed because of the discourses we had every evening. The Teacher was talking about morality and so many good things and I had seen exactly the other extremes—drugs, alcohol, you name it, which are part of this glamorous profession.

I cried a lot on the fourth and fifth days. Luckily I was able to talk to the assistant teacher about what I was feeling and she gave me masses of support and good advice. As the days passed by my questions grew fewer. It was amazing. Every time I had questions they would all be answered as I listened to the discourses.

I was also improving in meditation. I would look forward each day to going to the hall to meditate and to hear the discourses. All this was so new to me. Life started looking very bright and clear. I didn't even know when I got out of my depression. I started getting all the solutions. My anxiety went away. There was no confusion any more. I also stopped blaming everybody else and disliking them for whatever they had done to me.

There were also many times when I could not concentrate or keep the thoughts out of my mind. Initially I started getting very angry and agitated because I was scared that if I don't achieve this in ten days I will go out and be miserable again. Then I realized that it will take some time. I should relax. So whenever apart from group sittings I felt distracted, I used to get up and go out for five minutes and come back. I thought I should be happy that at least I have found the medicine. Now it's in my hands to continue the practice.

Coming to Vipassana was a miracle for me. It has saved my life. And I am so grateful to all the teachers and Dhamma servers who helped me get through this successfully. The day I came here is the most unforgettable day in my life and being able to remain here for ten days is a bigger achievement than any other title that I have won. It has once again brought back my confidence and courage. I am almost grateful that I was so miserable because otherwise I wouldn't ever have thought about coming here.

—*Madhu Sapre*

🐚

I realized how caught up I was in my own little world of all the egocentric things, trying to make myself happier, just for myself . . . I was giving to other people, but not without expecting something in return . . . .

There was a very quiet compassionate support in the wings and that was very reassuring . . . .

I mixed well with all the others. Everyone's so easygoing, so cooperative . . . .

I think it's well organized . . . wonderful that people who meditate here come back to give service and become part of it, because it keeps the feeling so alive. Everything just seems to fall into place.

—*Excerpts from postcourse interviews with first-time students, Australia 1990*

🐚

My friends had thought it funny that I, an incessant talker, was going to be silent for ten days. In fact that was not a difficulty. On the tenth day of the course we were allowed to talk. When I discussed the course with other students I was surprised to discover that the subtle body sensations were present all the time without any effort on my part. In rapid succession I was confronted by the effects of certain habits that I had developed and which I had varying degrees of awareness of before. When I interrupted someone I had one sensation, when I had critical thoughts about what someone was saying I had another, and when I talked too much without being sensitive to others a third body sensation occurred. These were rapidly established as reliable indicators and before long I was able to stop myself whenever I began to do these things.

—*Ron Thompson, New Zealand*

The actual experience of taking a course and just reading or talking about it are very different things. The actual experience of allowing oneself to take ten days off from our busy lives and just live like a monk or a nun in noble silence is something words alone cannot describe. The fact that total strangers are living, eating and meditating side by side for such an extended period of time in such peace and harmony is very hard to find anywhere else.

—Eva Sophonpanich, a Swedish national living and working in Thailand, sat her first Vipassana retreat in 1990.

During the course the door to the inner world, the world of my sensations opened, making the picture whole. Knowing such obvious things as "I should be good to people. I should be kind. I should generate only love and peace," is often not enough to apply them in everyday life. Now it seems to me that I've got the tool that can make it possible.

—Galina Ryltsova, a translator, wrote these comments after sitting a course in Moscow, Russia in summer 1998.

When the course finished on the morning of the eleventh day, the servers asked if we could help tidy up. This was a precious moment. For ten days they were our loving parents and now the time had arrived—we could "fly." We were "old students" and if we had the goodwill to donate our time we could do for others what they had done for us.

—Heather Downie, wife and mother of two, first encountered the technique at the Tasmania Vipassana Center, Hobart, Australia. She is a registered nurse and works part-time in a nursing home.

❧

Doing the cleanup jobs following the final breakfast with my Dhamma brothers and sisters was a great joy as was recrossing the Rocky Mountains with two different course members, a father and son who also happened to be Farrells. This was the second of his children the father had introduced to Vipassana. His son had been drifting— twenty-two years old with no clear focus. The course, he said, had given him an absolute direction. Everything seemed clear and simple to him now.

And guaranteed to change.

It had been hot during those ten early spring days in the foothills. Flood warnings were up, sand bags were being laid in low-lying areas, and those "eternal" peaks were bound to fall under the waves once again given enough days and nights, enough snow and wind.

Just observe, I told myself as we crossed from east to west and as I, too, headed for a new life.

Just observe.

—Jason Farrell, Canada

Chapter 5

THE COURSE EXPERIENCE—AFTER

Vipassana is an art of living. Once someone has sat a course they will know the basics of the technique and have enough personal experience to be able to decide whether the practice suits them. The purpose of Vipassana is always practical—to apply the benefits of meditation in real life. We go to a hospital for treatment, to recover strength and improve our physical condition. Likewise we come to a Vipassana course, not for a holiday or socializing or as an escape but to equip ourselves to deal more effectively with daily situations and improve the quality of our life. Not that we become perfect by taking a course. Beware of unrealistic expectations! The habit patterns we've unwittingly created over the years can be very resistant.

Back again in everyday life, facing the same problems and pressures as before, we can't run off somewhere quiet to remember what we learned on the retreat. Fortunately however, that plunge deep inside ourselves will come to our aid. Perhaps we still react to various unwanted situations but now less violently than before and for a shorter period. This itself is a major achievement. If we maintain a daily meditation practice, it soon becomes possible to remain aware of the breath and the sensations, so that when some crisis arises a part of the mind can observe our own reactions without being totally overpowered by external circumstances. To our surprise and delight, we find a shock-absorber has been installed, a wonderful deconditioner for the mind.

Now that we have returned to the big wide world, how do we build on what's been gained and keep growing on the path? Just as it was during the course, our commitment to maintaining the practice and working correctly is essential for success. Expect difficulties—after all, we are no longer in the protected atmosphere of the course—and become expert at overcoming them. The technique of Vipassana is clear, logical, nonsectarian, experience based, producing nothing but good for the individual and society. But still, unfounded criticisms might come. All the old suspicions, especially in the West, about meditation and those who get involved in it may surface. Explanations will go only so far towards convincing doubters that the practice of Vipassana is a healthy development. The way we live our lives and the positive changes we can bring to them will have a far greater impact.

We try to practice morality, concentration and purification of mind (Pāli: *sīla, samādhi, paññā*), not just in our meditation but wherever possible in our regular activities too. This requires willpower on our part to create some new routines and it requires acceptance by others of changes in us which they may not immediately welcome. "Hey!" the crowd might say. "Why don't you just forget all that meditation nonsense and have some real fun for a change. What you need to be happy is a good party—a few beers inside you, a few pills, a few smokes and pull a partner for the night." And so, here we have it: conflicting models of our prospective lives, of our very self, standing eyeball to eyeball. How will it turn out? Only we can decide, every time. It takes wisdom and strength of character to resolve these contrary forces. Daily sittings themselves often provide the routes through such dilemmas, but there is no easy formula.

Sorting out the practicalities helps. At home, finding a quiet, comfortable place to meditate without disturbance is a must. It helps to fix more or less regular times in our daily program for sitting. We try to practice properly, remembering the basic principles of awareness and equanimity, and if we forget it all or get stuck, we can always get a teacher's guidance. But each individual is his or her own master; there is no gurudom in Vipassana. We have to meet the challenge of keeping up our meditation and applying the teaching in everyday life alongside normal work and family commitments.

Meditators should evaluate their own progress on the path using various criteria, such as:

• Instead of hurting others, have I started helping them?

• How am I behaving in unwanted situations—am I reacting as before or am I remaining more balanced?

• Am I becoming less self-centered, giving generously without expectation of anything in return, showing compassion, developing gratitude towards those who help me?

• Am I establishing my meditation on a sound foundation by keeping the moral precepts day to day?

We will make mistakes, of course. The test is whether we can learn from them. Rather than creating new tensions, can we smilingly acknowledge our blunders and attempt not to repeat them?

We participate in and enjoy life to the full, understanding in high times and low that change is bound to come. We cannot stop the flow of events but we can influence their direction. When elation or depression come knocking, Vipassana helps us keep a level head. And this detachment does not mean passivity or indifference to suffering; watching and waiting, even for a split second, before acting actually makes for a more creative contribution. We become more capable of tackling tricky situations with calmness and confidence, kindness and good sense. The path is ultimately a solitary one but we do not walk it alone. Friendship born of compassion is at the heart of Vipassana. There are so many ways to get support for our own practice and to help others. Weekly sittings with other local meditators or weekend retreats recharge our batteries. Volunteering service, for instance on a course or at a center, is the greatest gift of our time and skill. Worldwide the network of Vipassana contacts is extensive and expanding. Everywhere—from Ulan Bator to Texas, Taipei to Milan, Johannesburg and Mumbai—the principles, the practice and the format of the teaching is the same. Via the internet the virtual community of Vipassana is just a keystroke away. Meanwhile real communities of families and friends are growing up around the retreat centers themselves—those rare places dedicated solely to meditation and service.

In brief, I'd say that I've had ten days of discovery. This course was like a key that opened a door to the real truth, real happiness, real understanding. To me the most important advantages of Vipassana are that it gives us an opportunity to experience the law of nature in ourselves and it is also easy to practice. The door is open and now I have to make my first steps on the way to myself. I hope my will is strong enough to keep on practicing . . . I thank my fate for giving me Vipassana!

    —*Marianna Igelnik, age 19, is a medical*
student in Moscow.

I have practiced Vipassana meditation every day for three months now. The rewards are great. The change in my life is enormous. I used to drink alcohol every day to survive the stress, now I can live without it. I was having a lot of trouble with my son, but since I learned not to react, not to get too angry, the relationship has taken a positive turnaround. I used to get a lot of headaches and take a lot of Panadol. I don't get so many headaches now, and I can, most of the time control them with regular meditation. I can get more done in a day because by clearing my head I have a clearer view of life.

Right now I am pushing myself to live in the here and now. Worrying about tomorrow was causing me stress and wasting valuable time. It's like being a child again, there's this feeling of timelessness. I used to think I could never afford two hours every day just to sit and meditate. I'm finding now that I can go to bed an hour later and get up an hour earlier so the time is not the big issue that I believed it would be.

—Heather Downie, Australia

The Buddha taught that we must not have blind faith in his words. Instead, we should discover their truth for ourselves. So I realized at my first ten-day course that I would have to determine if Vipassana meditation really works, if it really helps me reduce misery and develop equanimity. I didn't have to wait long for a test.

I worry a lot about lack of money. If there is one area of my life that I could use a little more equanimity, it would definitely be financial. When I was checking out of my first Vipassana course, I had the chance to see the effects of this meditation in action.

I had been wary of turning my wallet over to the registrar when I first checked into the course. Although I was given a plastic bag and masking tape to wrap and seal it in, I watched anxiously as the valuables box in which my wallet was placed sat unattended for much of that first afternoon. Ten days later, when I went to retrieve my wallet, I can't really say I was that surprised when I found that it wasn't in the box.

I was surprised by my reaction to the loss though. No intense anxiety. Yes, I was concerned, and I was glad that a young man offered to trace the valuables box back to its source in another room. Even when he returned five minutes later with empty hands, I noticed that I still felt pretty calm. When I began giving myself a hard time about entrusting my wallet to the box and worrying about how to replace my various credit cards and license, I washed some dishes and watched the thoughts go by. My mind stayed pretty clear. I remembered that the valuables box looked different than it had ten days earlier. Sure enough, after another ten minutes of searching, the young man returned with my wallet. The valuables had been transferred out of one box and into a second, and my wallet had been left behind.

It isn't always quick and easy to evaluate the results of Vipassana practice. But I think little events pop up along the way to give us insight into our progress. The road to liberation is long, Goenka says. But each step along the path is worthwhile. Is all of my anxiety about lack of money gone? Not by a long shot, but every experience of being more equanimous encourages me in my practice.

—Barry Nobel, a mediator and teacher, took his first course at the Northwest Vipassana Center, Washington, USA in 1998. As a postscript he adds: "I remain amazed that Vipassana produces enough worthwhile results that I still devote two hours daily to sitting."

When 1994 turned into 1995, I was sitting my first ten-day Vipassana course in Dhamma Mahī, France. I found the course quite hard and confronting, but also, especially afterwards, highly inspiring. I knew I had come into contact with something I had been looking for, yet without knowing it. There was also a strong realization that this meditation technique would likely be with me all my life, and I wanted to get firmly established in it.

When a course is coming to a close, Mr. Goenka advises his students that, if they find this technique logical, result oriented and beneficial, they should practice one hour in the morning and one in the evening, so I also started meditating like this when I got back home. For half a year, sometimes struggling, I managed to sit these two hours, and I kept on getting good results. I was less irritated, my concentration was better, which helped me when studying, and I found it easier to deal with the fifty-six other students in the housing complex.

In the summer of 1995 I flew to Bangkok, to start a two month trip through southern Thailand, Malaysia and Sumatra after which I would return to Thailand to sit my second Vipassana course at Dhamma Kamala just before returning to Holland. But after six and a half weeks of travelling, and feeling very open towards everyone I met, my trip came to a premature and most unexpected close.

One morning in Sumatra I went for a walk after meditating. I was joined by three Indonesian young men, who socialized a bit, asking me for my name and origin. They walked along with me, until we had left the village far enough behind, and then I wondered why my head was exploding. I couldn't see anything any more, and just felt very intense sensations on my head. When I got my sight back, I saw that the three had spread out, and that one of them had hit me on the head with a big stick he had picked up. Then I realized I was being robbed. They beat me some more and after frightening minutes my hands and feet were tied. Bleeding heavily I was put in the bushes beside the road. Then they left.

For a brief moment I accepted the fact that this was the moment I would die. But then there was a very strong push, an impulse from within, which made me continue. I realized that my head wound needed treatment rapidly, and also that my attackers could still come back. And at that very moment, when I could have been completely absorbed by the situation, something happened which gave me a moment of rest at a time I needed it most. I untied my hands and feet, and for a short time I just sat there beside that road, practicing Vipassana. I was aware of the sensations on my body, and maintained equanimity towards them, realizing they were just arising and passing away. I understood that, though the sensations were intense, they would not last forever and this allowed me to observe them instead of being overpowered by them. After a while, I started moving and thinking of ways to solve the troublesome situation I was in. I was found by other travellers, who helped me most wonderfully, and I was repatriated to Holland where I could recover. When those people had found me, one of them started cursing the boys, but the practice of Vipassana enabled me to feel nothing but sincere compassion for them. Their lives must be full of negativity, aggression and greed and I felt really sorry for them. What they did was absolutely wrong, and if possible, I thought, they should be punished for their deeds. Yet I was aware that by feeling hatred towards them, I would also be full of negativity, which would definitely not help me at this time when I needed all my energy to bring the situation to a good end.

Of course, back home, aggression came, hatred came, desire for revenge came, rage came, sadness came; I'm definitely not an enlightened person! But still all this time there were moments of equanimity, of facing the situation with a balanced mind. And these moments have been so helpful; they are invaluable! Now, with psychiatric treatment, I had to work for a year or more to be freed from the stress and the problems I had generated in reaction to this robbery. I can only imagine how much more time and effort it would have cost me, had I not been supported by Vipassana. At times in this first year after the robbery it was too hard to meditate, even Anapana. Yet the fact that the meditation had been so incredibly helpful and the results so enormous after only one course and half a year of regular practice—this ensured that I would come back to it.

When the time was right I sat a second course. When the retreat was over a fellow student asked me what kind of results I was getting so far. I answered him in vague, broad terms that it was helping me in various ways. He somehow kept coming back to this question, and I kept avoiding a specific answer. Just before the last day was over, and we were all going to bed, he asked me: "OK, just give me one example of a situation in which Vipassana has been beneficial to you." I then told him this story, and he understood the source of my inspiration.

—At age 24 Teun Zuiderent from the Netherlands has an M.A. in Arts & Sciences and an M.A. in Science & Technology. Job offers are on hold until he has completed a year of sitting, serving and studying Pāli at the Vipassana International Academy, Igatpuri, India.

What have I gained from practicing Vipassana?

As a result of observing the nasal and ear passages my sinuses have become much clearer and I can smell many things which I have not smelt in decades. A walk up the road a couple of days after the course was a delight.

I am now very much more aware of previous bad habits in relation to talking and listening and can mostly catch these quite quickly. Some situations are still quite difficult in this regard but I remind myself that all things can change.

My driving has slowed down by about 20 km/hr (12 mph), which pleases my wife. I am much more patient with other drivers and much more often look for the possibility to be generous with people who want to change lanes or get out of side streets. I get body sensations if I become impatient or inconsiderate in my driving.

I have steadily attacked piles of papers lying around the house and completed or begun jobs which I have long procrastinated over. Some of these seemed like huge mountains and required a lot of courage and persistence, but I began to do these things today instead of tomorrow. Every day I do something towards tidying up old messes and mostly catch myself when I am about to create a new one. I have become much more considerate of my wife in the things that I do around the house.

In my new found zeal I have at times made mistakes, sometimes quite big ones. This has lead to some suffering, but eventually I realize that I am craving or avoiding something and I am able to move on from the mistake. My impulsiveness and impatience are still there to some extent but it feels like they are diminishing with each painful lesson.

Talking with friends and relatives has been much more about real issues rather than avoidance of these. I have tried to temper my enthusiasm and allow my new calmer disposition to be present, listening more and not judging, often knowing things about people before they tell me and knowing when to hold back also. In some cases when others are speaking very critically about third parties then I feel distressed and find it difficult to remain equanimous. This will require further concentration or the prevention of such situations.

There are many things that I have worked out by the intellect in my life, as I generally have not had faith in the teachings of others. Vipassana has allowed me to directly experience so many things that it has truly created an entirely new reality, or should I say that it has dispelled many illusions. This has not always been comfortable and I know that further discomfort lies ahead but I now feel firmly established in continuing, to keep on taking one more step down that road. There have been periods of doubt and confusion, particularly involving the fact that my wife is practicing a different technique. It seems that I am finding an acceptance of this now but I also know that there may be some more lumps in the system.

Learning Vipassana has been the greatest gift I have ever received and my life has been changed so much that it can never be the same again. I know that I will give assistance to others who also want to take this ride but otherwise the future seems so much less certain than it did before. Who knows what tomorrow will bring?

—Ron Thompson, New Zealand

After I did my first course in April '97, I felt that by getting Vipassana I was more privileged, much more privileged than if I had won the lottery! Having since done a few more courses, I haven't changed my mind.

—Sheila Kirwan from London is a secondary
school teacher of math and science.

When I went back to work, most people recognized and appreciated my change. They said I was less aggressive (even though they used to consider an aggressive lady could manage the work better). They found out that by becoming less aggressive, I could achieve more. My professional environment became less tense and associates were more cooperative and cheerful. Being a patient and firm lady manager, I did not lose anything and gained more ease in working relationships. Dhamma provided me with guidelines such as if I want something to get done, better to do it myself rather than waiting and asking another person to do it for me with my mind in high agitation. When I do tasks which are not part of my job, like helping and showing others what to do, people are not "taking advantage" as I previously feared. Rather they do exactly what I want and tasks are done more quickly and efficiently. I remember Goenkaji's teaching "Set an example." Needless to say, I have to sacrifice my ego— "Why does an important person like me have to do such lowly work!" But as time's passed by, I have grown to love the low profile life style. I found the taste of peace within and I started to develop more harmony with others around me.

—Thanda Win, Myanmar

Where to begin—I feel I have gained so much from Vipassana. It is now twenty months since I did my first course, ten months since I decided to discipline myself to an hour's meditation twice a day and four months since my last ten-day course.

Since I began practicing two hours meditation each day, I have stopped smoking cigarettes and cannabis, I don't take alcohol and have stopped having caffeine. This may sound like a chore (it's not all strictly part of the technique) but being by nature quite an "addictive" person I feel set free from the constant craving for highs, nicotine, alcohol, food, sex and all.

I have become celibate since my first course (more or less), not out of self deprivation, but out of an inner calmness, of being freed from my tortures of lust and craving for sex, attention, mutual need, love. I don't necessarily intend to be celibate for ever (although if this is the case, it is OK) but I am prepared to wait until I find the right partner for me.

So that is what I have been able to do without.

Since doing Vipassana I have moved from being a staff nurse on an acute psychiatric ward to a charge grade psychiatric nurse working in the community. I find that I can concentrate more on people's problems and think more clearly. I can organize my day in an efficient manner and I have enough energy to keep going. If I find that I am flagging or I am being overwhelmed by the sheer volume of work, then I take ten minutes out to meditate and this is usually enough to calm my mind, give me energy and quite often find a solution to whatever difficulty has arisen.

Personally, I do not suffer the mood swings and the lows that were such a large part of my life before. If I do find myself having negative thoughts (I am much more aware of these now in their early stages, before they overwhelm me), I almost always remember that I had forgotten my sitting. If I then meditate, they go away again.

I am much calmer now. I don't get anxious about day to day issues and the anxieties I have about more major issues I deal with before they become a burden.

As a community psychiatric nurse, a large part of my job is to meet with and assess people who are basically going through the same lows, anxieties, out of control feelings, the same craving for sex, drugs, food and so on that I have been through myself. I consider myself very fortunate to have found a way out of this madness of endless craving and aversion. I find that I am filled with a great deal of empathy for what these people are going through and feel more qualified to help them because of it.

One day perhaps I can be part of a Vipassana center that helps people with the problems I see every day and week to week.

Vipassana has had a positive effect on every aspect of my life. I meditate for an hour before going to work and it leaves me with a calmness, clarity and energy. I meditate when I return home from work and I feel refreshed, the stresses of the day are gone. Again I find peace, my peace.

—*Tony White, UK*

On July 4, 1982 when Michael, from Ireland, was nineteen years old, he was involved in a serious motorcycle accident which left him with a fractured skull, a strained spine, a badly broken left leg and other less severe injuries. Two days later he lost the feeling in his body and became paralysed from the neck down. Michael spent the next few months in a rehabilitation center in Dublin. His walking recovered reasonably well during this period, although over the coming years on a few occasions he was described as an invalid because of his disability. To relieve some of the pain and try to overcome his difficulties with walking, Michael took a course in self hypnosis in 1985 but with little or no success. Some time later he began to buy books on meditation to learn more about the mind and in 1996/97 Michael went to the U.S. where he tried a number of different meditation techniques but found nothing that suited him. A healer friend in New York recommended Michael try Vipassana, saying he thought it would be good for his condition.

I sat my first course at the meditation center in Massachusetts and quickly took a liking to this very focused and one-pointed technique. But I faced a lot of difficulties. I had been spastic since my accident and trying to sit still during meditation, pain would arise in my legs which would trigger off spasms, causing the legs to jump. Whenever tension arose in my legs, I would move them as I always had done since the accident to try to avoid this reaction. When the legs were still my meditation was reasonably good, but once they started jumping or I needed to move them, the concentration was gone.

At the end of the course, I wanted just to get right back into this intensive meditation and develop it as much as possible as quickly as possible. However there was a shortage of volunteer workers at the center so I served the next two ten-day courses. Serving I found to be like sitting a mild course. One still gets the chance to sit in meditation at least three hours each day and watch the video discourse. One still gets to learn an awful lot about Vipassana.

During my second course, I got fed up with my spastic legs and the way they distracted attention away from meditation. By day six I had had enough of this problem and decided to try and totally ignore the tension, pain, spasms and just let the legs jump or do whatever they wanted to do. Whatever will be will be, I thought. For the rest of that day during meditation my legs continued to jump. Despite this, in a determined manner I tried to focus totally on that part of my body where I was observing sensations. When I got to my legs, I would just observe the discomfort as another sensation, even smiling at the discomfort there as if it was of totally no importance. Once I'd finished observing sensations in the legs, I would ignore this area and continue on to observe the rest of the body and associated sensations.

On day seven I continued to meditate in the same determined way. By now I began to notice that the tension arising in my legs was not as great as before. As the day unfolded the tension continued to decrease. By the day's end I was very glad I'd made that decision to ignore my spastic legs. For there was no more tension, no more spasms and my legs were still. It was only then I realized the importance of just being the observer and not reacting.

That night in bed I was able to relax straight away. Previously since the motorcycle accident, this would only be possible if my body was physically tired. Otherwise I would always be turning and twisting.

—Michael Egan, Ireland

Just several weeks ago we finished meditating for thirty days, and five months previous to that we had gotten married. And having had all that change in our lives— we'd both been single for a number of years—and to then get married and have that intensity of relationship . . . problems come up. Issues arise day by day and we deal with them. Certainly meditation helps in our daily life, but taking time to do a course separately and getting the clarity that comes from meditating for long periods and being able to look at our relationship with some objectivity, was so helpful. I just felt so grateful.

It's the best . . . to have this technique in a relationship is to have a tool that allows you to so clearly work out whatever two people in a relationship need to work out. You have that opportunity to go deeply inside and to understand how you yourself are causing the problems that might exist in the relationship. And you learn to stop passing those problems on. Still you do it. The old habit patterns don't go away instantly. This path does not cause any instant change per se, it causes a very strong steady change over time, as one practices properly.

And so Amanda and I find as a result, that we stop trying to blame the other person for any kind of problem. And we look inside ourselves and we find out why we might be having this problem, creating this tension in the relationship. And then, with that kind of honesty, that kind of look inside ourselves, then we have very open communication, and I don't think that she and I have any secrets from one another whatsoever. I don't think that there are any lingering tensions because we work them out continuously and the technique is an invaluable tool in doing that.

For instance, when you sit anything that might be just slightly wrong with our relationship comes up so strongly in the meditation. Comes up as sensation in the body as a burning or someplace you feel that tension because you become highly attuned to what's happening in the body. As we have found out from the meditation, the mind and the body are intricately connected. You cannot have a thought that doesn't have some sensation in the body. You can't have a sensation in the body that isn't strongly connected with thinking and feeling. So because you're so sensitive to this mind-body situation, you find that you just have to have these open discussions and clear the air quickly.

Certainly the divorce rate, which in our Western society is so incredibly high, is much less among established Vipassana meditators because people commit themselves for a lifetime in a way that a couple ought to commit themselves. And because of the technique, they can keep working out the problems instead of running away from them, as so often happens in our society—looking outside again, outside for somebody else, someplace else, to solve their problems. Meditators know that there's no place else to look but inside of yourself, so you learn to dive deep inside, find out where those problems are, and solve them as a couple.

—*In conversation, David and Amanda Crutcher*
from Massachusetts, USA

Since that first course, Tim and I have walked together step for step on the path. All of our relationships have improved and our old bad habits faded away. After that first course, I never smoked marijuana again because I never had a desire to do so. I could not conceive of clouding my mind with a drug after having worked so hard to clear it! Through consistent practice over the years, we have overcome most of the tension in our relationship, and certainly have a tool for dealing with it when it does arise. We often tell our family and friends that it is Dhamma that saved our marriage and it is Dhamma that keeps it strong. Today, we teach together in the same elementary classroom and spend most of our time together. Happily. Dhamma works!

—*Karen Donovan, USA*

. . . I'd just like to add that 95% of the initial appeal to people like me, when hearing of Vipassana, is the obvious integrity with which your organization and courses are run and funded. Thank you for making meditation (and a respected Teacher) both acceptable and accessible to the West, and, in particular, to my "socialist tradition."

—*Robert Byrne from southern England is training*
to be a homeopath and working part-time as a care
worker with the elderly. About radical politics he
adds: "I seem to be less involved in nonviolent di-
rect action these days, however the influence I now
exert on 'the bigger picture' by meditating, though it
may appear less, is undoubtedly more positive!"

VIPASSANA — CHANGING EVERYDAY LIFE

Chapter 6

ON THE PATH

Vipassana is intended to be applied in life. So far we've been concentrating on the meditation technique and how it's learned on courses. Now we're ready to shift the focus to real world situations—how it works across the spectrum, with children and families, with prisoners in jail, with addicts, with business people, professionals and others. As ever the individual is the starting point. So we begin this new section with meditators telling their own stories of transformation, from first sitting, through years of practice and service, to the responsibilities of teaching.

Sometimes a single Vipassana course can give someone enough direct experience of the truth inside that for them the path is clear: "This is where I want to go. This is what I want to be." For others it takes longer. Either way when we meditate daily, treat ourself and others right, then, bud to blossom, the inner change starts showing. Here are some snapshots from that memorable journey.

Dhamma

Sitting in the shadow of yellow-white light,
Illuminated in the glow of calm happiness:
I glimpse the way.

—Kathy Henry is a family nurse practitioner.
Together with her husband Ben Turner,
she has coordinated Vipassana courses
in a Seattle jail since 1997.

❧

First Course

Life prior to Vipassana was difficult for me. I was angry, anxious, self-pitying, unforgiving. I had spent many years living with an alcoholic on whom I blamed all my problems. And although to all outward appearances I seemed to be coping, my mind was filled with despair. I wanted what I couldn't have and was angry at the way my life had turned out. I was *suffering*.

I came to Vipassana through my son. At fifty-nine years of age, I didn't think there was much my children could teach me. Little did I know that my son was to give me such a great gift. I thought that I had given him the gift of life and now, here he was, giving it to me. He had travelled to India and done some volunteer work for the summer and afterwards did a ten-day Vipassana course before returning home. He spoke frequently and fervently of his time meditating at Dehradun and gave me William Hart's book *The Art of Living* to read. I decided that I needed a copy for myself and wrote to order one. With the book came a list of reading material and as I became more intrigued, I wrote to Dhamma Dīpa (the UK center) for more information and eventually took the giant step of registering for a ten-day course. I think my son became a little concerned at this point and reminded me over and over again of the 4:00 a.m. wake-up time, the ten hours of meditation a day and most of all the necessity to keep silent for nine days. I must admit this last point caused me a little concern as I am someone who "loves to chatter."

I was very hesitant when the big day arrived. I had visions of being encamped with a group of hippies, new age travellers and young people. The smiling girl who greeted me on arrival soon dispelled all my silly preconceived notions and in looking around the registration hall I saw people of all ages and descriptions. I felt comfortable from the first day.

My "cell-mate," as I liked to refer to the woman who shared my room, was as intent as I on getting the most out of those ten days so there was no problem with "rule-breaking chatter." In fact, this was one of the most enjoyable aspects—no need to converse unnecessarily.

It wasn't easy. I never thought I'd be able to sit comfortably, no matter which position I adopted or however many cushions I used. I experienced a lot of pain in my legs and standing up after one hour was pure agony. The period when we had to sit for two hours almost finished me off. But then, after several difficult days of trying to meditate, something happened. I woke one morning eager to get to the meditation hall. I was the first to arrive. I sat absorbing all the energy, all the Metta, all the peace. It was the start of some of the happiest days of my life. Some mornings, during rest periods, I watched the sunrise over the hills and in the evenings, marvelled at the sunsets. Every moment became special and even as these moments passed, as I learned to live in the present, accepting that "everything changes," my peace grew. I have never experienced such joy as on the tenth day of the course. It was the beginning and although stepping back into the modern world has subdued my joy somewhat, I still experience peace whenever I sit to meditate.

When my children were young and asked me what I wanted for my birthday present, I always said, "Just a little peace and quiet." In those ten days at Dhamma Dīpa, that is what I received.

I am only a beginner, I have much to learn. In my day-to-day life it is not always easy to practice "living in the present," to detach, to meditate. I am just now preparing to register for another ten-day course. I hope to go once a year. I am looking for a group to meditate with in my area on a weekly basis.

Each day as I sit to meditate I feel as if my life is changing, I am changing. I am learning and Vipassana is my teacher.

I read a quotation once which begins "Place yourself in the middle of the stream of power and wisdom which flows into your life." Vipassana meditation is my stream. What have I gained from practicing Vipassana? The truth about myself and the beginning of liberation from suffering (and I don't "chatter" nearly as much).

—*Jean Bayne is retired and lives in southwest England.*

&

A Clue and a Gift

During a time of profound metaphysical crisis, I was attempting to keep the external parts of my life in some kind of functioning mode. A part of this was my membership on a committee which I was highly committed to in principle, though the contact it necessitated with one of the chief movers and shakers was always challenging for me. We were two people with a diametrically opposed way of looking at, speaking about and living our lives. I had also undertaken some training as a potential volunteer phone counsellor, in order to put some meaning into my seemingly aimless life.

If I had had a strong religious conviction, a long retreat, like six months worth, might have seemed like the possible way to get myself back on the road again. However the strong church upbringing of my youth had been forced upon me, and had held no real meaning for me for twenty years. Undertaking such a retreat would have been plainly hypocritical and therefore useless.

Being a great believer in the role of the local library in the overall scheme of human existence, I went there one day to search for a clue. I found a couple of books in the Religion and Philosophy section which told of two different people's experiences in Thailand and Burma involving a meditation technique which sounded both harrowing and uplifting. Deep inside, I knew I was onto something productive, and this discovery alone gave my life a little more impetus.

The next day, I had to pay a visit to the committee rooms to complete some important paperwork. The person in question was there, waxing lyrical as often, about some trauma that had left a deep imprint in the form of an acute stomach ache. Against my intuitive need to be away from this overwhelming negativity, I found a part of myself that was able to squeeze out a drop of compassion. Using my newly developing counselling skills, I asked "What would you like to do with this pain in your stomach?" Walking towards the window and going through the appropriate actions, my colleague replied "I'd like to screw it up in a ball and throw it out of this window! Oh it's gone, it's gone. Oh thank you, thank you!"

As a way of repaying me for this act which I didn't feel very much responsibility for, I was shown a recently arrived new pair of shoes—exquisite soft leather pumps, made with extraordinary skill and decorated in painstaking and understated style. I was quite taken aback at their beauty. On asking where they came from, I was told, "Someone my brother meditates with made them." As though treading barefoot around a floor strewn with broken glass, I made enquiries about what kind of meditation. Though my colleague was clearly not in the least bit interested in her brother's bizarre hobby, a brief explanation sufficed to let me know that this was the same technique I had just been reading about. The brother's phone number was carefully elicited.

A phone call that day confirmed that yes this was the same Vipassana technique I had read about. I was given the phone number of Dhamma Bhūmi in the Blue Mountains, just outside Sydney. On ringing them, I discovered that a ten-day course was due to start very soon and that I was able to attend.

That first course healed the deep wounds I had been carrying for so long, and a long way off, at the end of the tunnel, was the possibility of a more fulfilling way of life, beyond mere religion. I have often pondered on this chain of events, and thought how appropriate that the gift should have been given to me because I was able to momentarily overcome my deep aversion to the behavior of someone and give to them.

> *—Olivia Salmon has made her home in New South Wales, Australia. Though not always keeping up her meditation since the retreat in 1988, she tries to live by its principles. Maintaining an awareness that, "This too will change," she's convinced, helped her recover from a life threatening horse riding accident in 1990.*

Journey to the East 1972

John Beary comes from the United States but has lived and worked in Japan for seventeen years as a college instructor. He and his wife were among the first generation of Westerners to learn the technique directly from S.N. Goenka in India.

I find it very curious that now in my fiftieth year I've been practicing Vipassana meditation for more than half my life. Twenty-five years ago my wife Gail and I began a journey to the East that would turn out to be a transforming one in every sense of the word.

Someone once said that your education only begins when you start to travel. Ours commenced a few weeks after our marriage in 1972 with a flight to Europe. With an eye eastward we slowly meandered southward to Spain, took a boat out of Barcelona to Egypt, visited Lebanon, Syria and Iraq, and wound up a couple of months later in Kuwait hoping to find passage on a ship to Bombay. We had read somewhere of a ship that left from Kuwait for Bombay calling at ports in the Persian Gulf. This sounded like just the ticket as it was now January and the overland route to India via Iran and Afghanistan would be too cold for us without winter clothing.

The SS Dwarka was a P&O Line ship built in 1948 as an unberthed passenger ship. This meant that although it offered a few cabins it was designed to serve deck class passengers, steerage in other words. It sailed the Persian Gulf between Basra and Bombay and mostly served the Hajis making the pilgrimage to Mecca. (In the movie "Gandhi," in the scene where the Mahatma arrives back in India from South Africa, that newly painted white ship was none other than the seaworthy SS Dwarka, which safely delivered not only Ben Kingsley but also Gail and myself to India's shores.)

Since the cheapest cabin class on the SS Dwarka was a whopping ten times the price of deck class, Gail and I paid our $40 and were counted among the unberthed passengers. We would not be dining at the captain's table on this voyage! Along with two intrepid Italians we found ourselves crammed below decks with about 900 Arabs and Pakistanis bound for ports in the Gulf and/or Pakistan. Cold seawater showers and the hottest curries imaginable (to this day) were nicely offset by a kind crew of British and Chinese seamen. They took pity on Gail who couldn't eat a bite of the fiery fare by supplying her cheese and bread from their own canteen.

The journey that was supposed to take nine days wound up taking eleven as we made lazy stops in the Persian Gulf at Bahrain, Doha, Dubai, Muscat and then onto the Pakistani ports of Gwadar and Karachi, before steaming into Bombay (now Mumbai) on the 6th of February, 1973.

"Why India?" my mother repeatedly asks me

It's an often-repeated question. In a sense, India is the ancient teacher of humanity. It is the spiritual home of two of the world's great faiths, Hinduism and Buddhism, which have each had such transforming effects on generations of visitors: conquerors, colonists, traders, travellers and tourists alike. A land imbued with spiritual heights of fantastic vision dovetailed next to deep ignorance and superstition. A magical land where possibilities exist of entry to worlds unimagined. Certainly India is one of the most otherworldly places on this earth. A timeless place, India is a must-see destination for all seekers.

"Visit India," the Air India Poster in Baghdad said, "you'll never be the same again." Truer words were never spoken.

Was there ever a time, before or since, like India in the early 1970s?

India at that time was going through another of its many invasions as droves of young Westerners now flocked to it. A resurgent interest in things Eastern—philosophy, spirituality, music, not to mention cheap living and an unbelievable degree of unbridled freedom—made the subcontinent an attractive destination for a wide variety of young Westerners.

In those days British young people would set off hitchhiking to India with 50 pounds sterling in their pocket and spend months sampling life on the subcontinent. For North Americans in a hurry, Air India at that time was offering round trip flights to Delhi from New York for $450. Many people went straight from college campuses and/or rock festivals to sample the giddy heights of the mystic East. However, without time to culturally decompress, many found the streets of village India to be somewhat more than they had bargained for. The Air India ticket required a minimum stay of 30 days before the return flight could be used and there were many tearful negotiations at the Air India office in New Delhi for those wanting out early.

Those travellers who had acclimated to West Asia via the overland route from Europe through Turkey, Iran, Afghanistan and Pakistan were weary but seasoned travellers by the time they reached India. They fared better and found in India a welcome change from the countries they had passed through. India has an atmosphere of tolerance and freedom seldom encountered elsewhere.

On the overland route to India as well as within India itself young Western travellers would frequently meet at crossroads, share a bus ride or an evening's lodging and then without design meet thousands of miles and weeks later as their paths crossed once again. Exchanging information on places visited, places to avoid and things to do, this eclectic network of young backpacking nomads included many who were attracted to the early Vipassana meditation courses taught by S.N. Goenka. News of Goenkaji and the Vipassana courses spread almost entirely by word of mouth with the result that literally thousands of young people attended those early courses across the length and breadth of India in the early 1970s. Some would follow Goenkaji from course to course, taking a number of consecutive courses before heading home or to different shores. Some remained in India for years and got involved with serving on the courses. It was these individuals, the handful of early Dhamma servers, who would play such an important role in the beginning days of Dhamma Giri, the first meditation center at Igatpuri.

Contact

As the SS Dwarka steamed into Bombay harbor, on the east side of the peninsula the Gateway of India seemed to be welcoming us just as it did England's King George V on his state visit to India in 1912.

Setting foot for the first time on Indian soil was exhilarating. After eleven days at sea, here we were in India! Down the gangplank, through Indian Customs and into a horsedrawn carriage— even King George couldn't have felt grander. We were giddy, flushed with excitement at finding ourselves on the threshold of the vast subcontinent, the land of the Buddha, yogis, Gandhi, Kipling. That first night in Bombay we met a British traveller at our guest house in Colaba who, upon hearing that we had just set foot in India said, "Don't miss taking a Goenka meditation course while you're here." When I asked what kind of meditation "Goenka" was he said "Oh, it's a meditation on the metabolic processes of the body." So much for factual descriptions from old students. . . . With that nebulous response I discounted the idea, thinking that here in the mystic East there would be countless techniques of meditation to sample. Little did I know at that time that I would sample only one of them and remain content with it all these years.

We soon left Bombay's urban commotion for the quiet beaches of Goa, looking forward to rest and relaxation after three months of hard travelling. Another ship and another day at sea and we arrived in Panjim, Goa. We headed to Colva Beach a few kilometers outside the town of Margao. Less crowded than the infamous hip Arjuna Beach, Colva was quiet by comparison. There were a number of rooms for let in the seaside village but we opted for a grass shack on the beach. A twelve year old boy who was to become our first landlord had recently constructed it. He was a hard bargainer and we finally settled the rent at 100 Indian rupees per month (about $8).

We weren't long in Colva before we met a Vipassana old student who was able to shed a little more light on this "Goenka meditation." I remember the young woman well and credit her for "turning us on to Vipassana." To this day, though we've lost contact with Sandy Snyder, we always remember her. She had taken, I think, two courses with Goenkaji and, while she didn't describe much that I can remember about the course, there was something about her recollections that touched me. She recounted her own misgivings about getting involved with cults and mysticism. Without a trace of preaching she recounted the no nonsense discipline the course required, what a struggle it was to try to control her mind and the solid benefits she felt she earned as a result. It was just what I wanted to hear: that development of mind was possible and that the only cost was honest effort, not blind belief. When I heard that the next course was about to begin in a few days in Bombay, I was ready to return there immediately for it. Gail persuaded me to register instead for the following course in Madras in early April, which we did by writing the next day to the registration contact asking for a place on the upcoming course at Ram Kalayan Mandapam.

In the meantime we had time to rest and enjoy a couple of weeks in Goa. Afterward we made a quick journey across south India to Rameswaram, where we boarded a ferry to Ceylon. After a hurried two weeks on the island we arrived back in India in Madras, a mere ten days early for the meditation course we were determined not to miss.

Meeting a remarkable man

One of the first things we did in Madras was to track down the registration contact for the course, a local businessman, Mr. K.C. Toshniwal. He was quite surprised to find two bedraggled road-weary Westerners at his office door. More would follow though, as the course attracted about 100 of our tribe. We also learned that shortly before the course Goenkaji would give a public talk on Vipassana and we made plans to attend.

The talk in Madras was in a section of the city that tourists and travellers were not likely to frequent. With difficulty we somehow managed to find the hall and waited with a few other young travellers and about fifty Indians for Goenkaji to arrive. He came in shortly and after a few silent minutes began speaking in Hindi. He went on in Hindi for some time and I began wondering if he was going to speak to us few foreigners in English at all. Finally after about an hour he began in English and explained to us what we were about to undertake in our first Vipassana course.

Though the years have blurred the details of that first talk I remember it mainly for its clear, down-to-earth presentation and its absence of mysticism. U S.N. Goenka, as he was known then, came across as the genuine article. His sense of humor and self-deprecating lack of airs found a receptive audience in us. We left the hall feeling positive. So far, so good; we were on the right track and looking forward to the course beginning in a few days.

First course, Madras 1973

The course site was Ram Kalayan Mandapam, a small marriage hall in a suburb of Madras. It was quiet enough from the front but the rear of the two-story building abutted a market street where the daily bazaar sounds provided the backdrop to the course. We arrived early in the day the course was to begin and as others began to arrive we found familiar faces from the road among them. In all, about 140 students took the course with the majority being young Western travellers. We were shown floor space to lie down. No mattresses, no sitting cushions, no mosquito nets. Unlike today's comfortable courses, in those days it was bare bones; if you didn't carry it with you, you went without. Toilet and bathing facilities were designed for much smaller gatherings, which meant a near-continuous queue during the break times. And it was April—temperatures soared into the high 30s Celsius (upper 90s Fahrenheit).

The ten-day course format was the same then as it is today: Anapana, maintaining awareness of respiration, for the first three and a half days, and then the practice of Vipassana for the remainder. The daily timetable was the same, with the addition of hot milk and fruit at 9:00 p.m.

Goenkaji was a very energetic teacher in those days. He gave two discourses, Hindi and English, each day, led every group sitting, conducted checking, gave noontime interviews and held a lengthy question-and-answer session each evening which lasted well past 10:00 p.m. Only years later, as a new assistant teacher, did I appreciate what an astonishing effort he put into those early courses. And yet he worked so joyfully. Here was a man who practiced what he preached and displayed the benefits of his practice in his every action. His instructions and explanations were so simple, so scientific and down to earth. There was no mysticism, no great leaps of faith; personal experience was the only criterion.

Goenkaji's message of what the Buddha taught was clear and pragmatic, free from dogma and dependence on any guru: each of us has only himself and the results of his actions to rely on, there is no outside agency he can petition for happiness or liberation. It struck a deep resonance within me for in the end it was simply common sense. Goenkaji's enthusiasm for this, the heart of the practice of Dhamma, was so full of joy that it was simply infectious. It often served to carry a wavering student over the difficulties of the course.

However there was no getting around the fact that the course required hard work. And I had mine cut out for me. I had heard that we would be required to sit on the floor more or less cross-legged. And that there would be sessions in which we were asked not to move for a full hour. Now, despite an athletic background, flexibility of the lower extremities was never my strong point and the mere prospect of sitting cross-legged for ten days was daunting. Sitting in that posture for a full hour was out of the question! A few days before the course, in our hotel I tried to see how long I could manage this sitting position and made it to fifteen minutes before collapsing in pain. Yet somehow on the course I was able to contend with the physical discomfort and incredibly found, after Vipassana practice began on day four, that with a strong determination I could complete each of the hour-long sittings without moving.

The levels of pain encountered and transcended were extraordinary. The dredging up of repressed memory and emotional pain accompanied them hand in hand. In turn they ebbed and flowed, as I tried to practice Vipassana and just observe what was taking place within me without the usual habit of reacting to it. With each experience of this ebb and flow of agreeable and disagreeable experiences it began to dawn on me that I was largely responsible for my suffering both physically and mentally. When pain arose I made it worse by fighting against it in the hopes of making it go away. When I learned to just accept it for what it was—a passing phenomenon—its entire temper altered. Not that I became insensitive to the pain but it no longer held the same sway over me. At times (for very brief moments) I was actually able to interrupt the anguish that normally accompanied it. These moments grew and I felt a real sense of gaining control over myself. In the short span of ten days I had gotten a glimpse of what was possible and began to consider: is there anything that a determined person can't attain?

Goenkaji said early on that the course was like an equation: you would get out of it exactly what you put into it. I took that advice to heart and made very strong efforts. By the end of ten days I had been through the most wrenching, cathartic experience of my life both physically and emotionally. It felt like a great purge had taken place within me and in its wake had left me strangely quiet and satisfied. I felt I had encountered a practice somehow vaguely familiar.

The benefits of that very first course and two more over the next couple of months were so profound that it took some time to be able to register and view them with perspective. One aspect however was immediately startling. The moral precepts we were asked to follow for the duration of the course had initially struck me as quaint and curious. Now at the end of the course I had realized directly their importance and from that very first course it has been easy to keep them unbroken in any major way. For me in those days this was no small thing. One of the precepts, though, required some elaboration.

One day late in that first course in Madras I went to Goenkaji at noon to let him know how I was doing and to give him my "take" on his teaching, the Dhamma. Though satisfied in general with his presentation, I thought that in my case I'd require an exemption or at least a more flexible attitude toward *sīla* (the moral precepts), especially the fifth one. But he would hear none of it, saying that even slight use of any kind of intoxicant was totally incompatible with the practice of Vipassana. When I went on and described my practice and said that I thought I might need a little more work on this technique he readily concurred, saying it sometimes took a couple of courses to get the hang of it. With that unambiguous direct invitation ringing in my ears I made up my mind to attend the next course two weeks later in Baroda, a city north east of Bombay.

It took a little while to persuade Gail what a good idea it was to take another course so quickly. And Baroda in May was no joke: water shortages, temperatures in the 40s Celsius (110s Fahrenheit) and the two of us the only foreigners on a Hindi-only course. But in the end all was worth it. With this second course completed we felt over the hump and happily headed off to Nepal to cool out for the remainder of India's hot season. After trekking in the Himalayas of Nepal we returned to India for a third course in Dalhousie in August before beginning the long journey home.

Search complete

I remember being asked a number of times during this peripatetic period just what it was that I was searching for. The question always seemed to annoy me, as if searching for something was somehow beneath me, as if it demeaned me in some way. What? Me need something? I'd react and protest that I wasn't searching for anything. But deep down I knew that while not on a formal search per se I was certainly on the lookout for something, anything, which was good and which would last. In its unrefined mode, that often meant being attracted to greater and greater doses of enjoyment or pleasure. But these temporary diversions never satisfied for long. At a deeper level there was an emptiness needing to be filled, a thirst that I knew sensuality would never be able to fully quench. When I completed my first course and then two more I felt satisfied beyond my wildest expectations.

From that time onwards I've felt an inner certainty that here in the practice of Dhamma was the good path, here in the practice of Vipassana was the development work that needed to be done in this lifetime. That thrill of the enthusiastic new student in 1973 has never long been absent from my mind these twenty-five years. Instead it has deepened with each succeeding step on the path of Dhamma and has sustained me without interruption. I consider myself the most fortunate person in the world for having found my way at such a comparatively young age. I feel so grateful for the efforts my teacher took on my behalf. Without him I don't know where I'd be today.

Next

In 1982 Gail and I were among those Goenkaji asked to represent him and conduct courses on his behalf as his assistant teachers. Initially I was reluctant until I began realizing that all I was doing was introducing newcomers to my teacher and his presentation of Vipassana. In effect I'm saying to them now what I said to many others way back then in India, "Hey, you've just got to meet this man and listen to what he has to say." Once when I explained this to Goenkaji he said that, yes, that's what he's doing too, continuing to assist his teacher Sayagyi U Ba Khin in introducing students to the practice of Dhamma just as he taught it. May all of you who read this take me up on this invitation and come and see for yourselves the benefits of this good path. May all of you be happy.

—John Beary, USA

ॐ

Embracing Life

Vipassana is a path, taught by the Buddha, that leads to *nibbāna*. First the word path—which is poetic and evocative—but what does it mean? I think the best colloquial translation of the word path is "a way of life." Vipassana is intended to be and was originally taught as a way of life. It doesn't have to be used in that way. Certainly there are people who come to a ten-day Vipassana course, get some value out of it, and never continue to practice or never return. We have, obviously, nothing against that and that may be valuable for some people. But the intention behind the teaching and the essence of the teaching is to help people establish a way of life. It's a path that leads potentially, from its origin when you first start practicing Vipassana, through the rest of your life.

Two other words that might help describe a path, or a way of life. One is that it's enduring. It's something that remains of value. I found, in life there are two kinds of activities. There are those that, the more you do them the less valuable they become. Many of the pleasures of childhood seem to become less relevant to adults. And then there are other activities which, the more you do them the more valuable they become. Enduring activities, classic ones would be reading or friendships, that have become increasingly valuable with time. So Vipassana is enduring.

And it's embracing. Embracing means that it's not focused simply in a narrow way. But it's focused outward. It sweeps into life and embraces many or even all aspects of life.

—Paul Fleischman, psychiatrist and writer;
an excerpt from a talk given to the 1999
Vipassana Conference held at Dhamma
Dharā, Massachusetts, USA

🐚

Psychology from the Inside

For as long as I can remember I believed that every person had the right, and the ability to achieve, peace and happiness. When it did not happen for me automatically, as all my childhood (and adult) fairytales had promised, I was lost. No one had given me any practical way of overcoming the pain and suffering that I was experiencing. This led me, as a mature adult, to turn to the study of psychology, to find the answers, to help myself and to help others to happiness.

After years of study the pain and disillusionment was multiplied rather than diminished. I remember looking around at my fellow students and realizing that these were the people who were now equipped to go out into the world as experts on the mind and human behavior, and supposedly to have the answers to help others. From numerous workshops, from exam results and from personal contact I knew that they did not know much more than myself. In fact, some very young ones probably knew less through a lack of life experience.

Then I considered our lecturers, those that had guided and worked with us through the years, who obviously knew their theories and had had a lot of experience. Some of them I had gotten to know personally and I knew that their marriages were in trouble, some had children with serious behavioral problems that they could not handle positively, some were just plain miserable and others downright ignorant in their attitudes and behavior.

For some time I was immobilized with disappointment and despair. Finally my determination, and faith in my belief of the existence of a way out of suffering, surfaced again. There had to be a way! Back to the books and a period of intense self education and examination. This time I studied the alternative approaches to mind and body healing. It seemed that I was getting closer but there were still missing links.

One thing that I knew for sure at this stage was that the old adage "Know Thyself" was an essential prerequisite of any personal growth, and of any possibility of helping others.

Would meditation help? Up until then I had resolutely avoided involvement with any groups with gurus, any groups that aimed at developing personal power over matter or mind, already understanding that one must retain full responsibility for one's own mind and that power corrupts if the ego is strong. Could I find a suitable practice in the swamp of alternatives?

A few tentative enquiries led me to Vipassana meditation as taught by Mr S.N. Goenka of India. When I first heard about this meditation I knew that it was important for me. In fact I felt it was familiar. But I also remember very carefully and very suspiciously studying the literature that was promptly forwarded to me. However it was with alacrity, still tempered by cautiousness, that I enrolled in my first course held in the Blue Mountains, west of Sydney.

Knowing the often exorbitant cost of workshops, psychology fees and the greed that was often involved in mitigating people's suffering, I was very impressed by the fact that these courses were being run on a donation basis and with voluntary workers. But what about the quality?

Ah, the relief to find that it was not a "hippie" outfit, that it was well organized, that there were people from all walks of life, and all ages there, that the management appeared intelligent and caring, that the facilities were clean and comfortable. Right until the end I was waiting for the financial hit, the hidden charges. It did not come. Everything was given unconditionally. We were only asked to follow rules and to surrender to the teacher's guidance. Much of that course was spent marvelling at the generosity that was being given so selflessly.

After all the preliminaries and formalities were completed, I resolved to put my intellect aside and to focus on the practice as it proceeded. All the best theories and scientific premises are of no use to us unless there is a positive gain to be had, especially on a long term basis. I worked as instructed, and worked and worked until I was a blur of exhaustion. The ten longest and most difficult days of my life unfolded slowly, and that is saying something, given some of the problems that I had experienced to date.

At the end of the course I had no idea what I thought or felt about the efficacy of the ten days that I had spent there. My whole being seemed to be in a state of shock from the intensity of the practice. For once my mind had surrendered to a position of observation, rather than theoretical analysis.

It was only later, in retrospect, that I understood that a profound change had taken place in my mind, my psyche. No other psychology technique or practice that I had come across had ever come close to bringing this sort of change. This was experiential change, deep change with an increased wisdom of my own to go with it. My wisdom, from my own experience, my own practice.

It came as a surprise to find not only myself at the next course, but also my husband. He had seen the changes in me and had realized that at long last I had perhaps found a gem. My memory of the difficulties of the previous ten days had faded with the excitement of the discovery of the effectiveness of Vipassana meditation. This time I resolved that I would work even harder and also try to understand the theory behind the practice. It was like a jigsaw puzzle, all the bits and pieces of understanding that I had, slowly began to connect together.

Within the year, my eighteen year old son also started working with Vipassana. He saw the positive changes in both of us and this inspired him to also take the plunge into self observation and wisdom. Not long after, my seventeen year old daughter, who had already experienced some of the difficulties and suffering inherent with growing up in a troubled society, undertook her first course. We were now a Dhamma family, all committed to work seriously on ourselves and to also help others achieve the same wonderful benefits.

—Marie Villesen sat her first retreat in 1984.
Together with husband Carsten, she gets great
satisfaction from working as a Vipassana volunteer
and enjoys exploring the Australian bush.

Colors

My name is Vanessa and I have been practicing Vipassana for three years. I was born in an African-American family forty-two years ago at Roanoke, Virginia, USA. Growing up in a segregated society influenced my views and perceptions on every level. I learned hatred, mistrust and resentment toward the white community. I didn't know any member of my community that privately didn't harbor these emotions, regardless of their social status. This position of professional victimization was a daily burden. I needed to find a way out. I was always searching for techniques, religions, philosophies that could offer me peace of mind. How could I love anyone, myself included, if I knew that I hated and feared this group.

I have lived in New York City for the past seventeen years. There I was fortunate to hear about Vipassana from a friend and I knew I had to try it.

My first course, I remember Mr Goenka talking about body sensations and how we react to them. I realized that this is what I had been doing and this activity would continue to hold me a prisoner to actual and perceived racism. Mr Goenka stated that life was misery but there was a way out. I didn't understand the technique in those first courses but I trusted that Vipassana would disperse the deep-rooted complexes I carried.

In the USA the only courses I've attended were at the center in Massachusetts. I am deeply moved by the dedication and hard-working energy of this Vipassana community. As I continued to take courses and serve as a volunteer there, I noticed that very few African-Americans participated. Many that did attend did not return and few, if any, had progressed toward longer retreats. I was frequently the only person of a colored background at the center; this position enabled me to observe quite acutely my aversion toward the white community. Emotions and thoughts long since buried surfaced again. Sitting course after course, practicing Vipassana, I noticed a change taking place in me. I was starting to feel a deep compassion for the white group whom I had once hated, and realized they were as much in misery and ignorance as I was.

My hatred, fear and jealousy toward them were lifted. For the first time in my life I could actually observe experiences related to racial issues more objectively and respond in a balanced fashion.

I have been telling members of my community about Vipassana. Many are excited and ready to take a course. I am going to make every effort to find off-center sites near the city.

> —*Vanessa Rawlings from New York wrote this account after completing a forty-five-day meditation retreat. Both her parents have sat a ten-day Vipassana course.*

🏵

Battling a Crisis

My youngest son Alex's death sent me into a major depression, but neither Lisa nor I recognized it at first because my sudden fits of anger blinded us to what was really going on. I was working very hard for the California Housing Trust, trying to keep it from being pushed into bankruptcy by its troubled projects, commuting 150 miles a day. I was manic and under lots of pressure from day one, and very fearful I would fail. I directed the anger at Lisa and the housing trust staff. Lisa took it for about a year and then told me we had to see a counsellor or I had to leave. So we went to a therapist who persuaded me to get antidepressants and then began to work with us on what was really my problem. The therapist worked hard to establish trust and rapport with me but was clear that this kind of anger was unacceptable. I started the medication, and it helped but not completely. I continued to blow up on occasion, so the therapist suggested I try meditation. A few months later, after I was fired, the time was available in spades, so I went.

I had learned about Vipassana from a colleague at the housing trust, but because of the workload I had, I never had the time for the ten-day training session. Coincidentally, I picked a course for the last part of August without thinking much about the fact that Alex's birthday is August 25.

It was very difficult. After the first day, I knew I was going to have trouble staying on. The silence wasn't so bad, but the pain in my body, my back and legs especially, from sitting was almost unbearable. Then, sometime during the fifth day, just as I was sure I would just have to quit, the pain dissipated almost entirely and quite suddenly in the midst of the afternoon group session. The tears started streaming down my face because I knew I had passed through some kind of barrier and that I would make it. And I did. It was not a piece of cake; there was still pain and lots of impatience, but I never had any doubt that I could finish the course.

I suspected, and believe today, that I was on the path to some kind of liberation. As the course went on, I grew happier—then in the final two days, positively exhilarated. When it ended I felt both sky-high and limp with relief.

The breakthrough with the pain was on the day before Alex's birthday, and when I told the teacher about this and my guilt over being a bad and absent father, she said simply that the exceptional pain could very well have been the pain I felt about his death having never been fully expressed. I think this is true, that the meditation allows me to focus on these feelings and releases the grief.

I don't pursue the cause and effect cycle too much because I don't have to. I'm at peace with the fact of his death, I'm not haunted by guilt or remorse or loneliness. I miss him terribly, but the idea of the young man he was lives on in my mind.

I'm happier than I have ever been in my life. I hardly ever lose my temper now and am quick to feel real remorse about it when I do, so I can apologize immediately. In one way, I don't recognize myself, but in another I do— I'm the guy I would have been in 1970 if I hadn't started drinking hard liquor daily in 1965. Lisa and I have the kind of marriage we always wanted. The companionship, the joint struggle toward our goals, are sufficient to make the marriage good—even excellent. I owe my life to her for getting me to AA which was the start down this path. The therapist was critical for insight, for the surface to use as a sounding board, for the intellectual engagement and the tough love encouragement, and the meditation was simply the most profound experience of my life, which completed the liberation from demons.

—*Wally Roberts, 58, is a community organizer*
and journalist in USA

🍃

A Quiet Space

On coming back from ten days serving on a Vipassana course, my shakuhachi teacher said: "What has happened to you? You are playing amazingly, as if you are not your usual self but someone else."

Shakuhachi is a Japanese end-blown bamboo flute. The way to play it is by placing the blowing edge on the upper chin so that the sharp edge will be centered in the air stream produced from one's lips. Structurally speaking it is a very simple instrument with only five finger holes, but it sends forth myriads of tones and shades. The distance from one's mouth to the tip of the blowing edge of the mouthpiece helps determine the pitch. One can raise the pitch by tilting the head down and bringing one's mouth closer to the edge of the mouthpiece.

Controlling the sound is a very difficult matter and involves producing a steady air stream and being able to control it in different ways. Every change in one's breathing is immediately reflected in the sound produced, thus making the shakuhachi a perfect mirror of one's own breath motions. A very sensitive mirror of one's inner emotional undulations. And mine used to be very shaky, a soul afraid of its own reflection.

By meditating on three Vipassana courses, serving one and sitting every day for two hours I gained many things. One of them is developing a kind of inner calmness, steadiness. An inner space, like a quiet lake, that whatever I am dealing with nowadays, be it people, work, thoughts or playing the shakuhachi, can be taken into this quiet space in me and dealt with peacefully.

And I feel that it is but a stage and the understanding and wisdom gained is continuously building up and spaces within me are widening constantly.

—Iris Elgrichi was born in Israel in 1961 and is currently enrolled in a literature doctoral course in Japan.

Learning to Balance

While the experiences that can arise in meditation are not to be compared nor given any valuation, still the relating of them sometimes helps to inspire confidence in others who are struggling on the same path. But if certain of these experiences are taken as something which one must attain, then they create obstacles. A few instances will illustrate the point . . .

In my tenth or eleventh course I found that I could not feel sensations below the nostrils and above the upper lip, nor anywhere else in the body for seven or eight days. No complaint. No advice sought. Just observe what is.

Once it also happened that after seven or eight years of meditation, having taken a number of courses and assisting Goenkaji with the teaching work, there arose in me during one course a tremendous aversion to the discipline, rules and regulations. It began the first day at the first sitting and was so strong that it was not possible for me to do a single moment of Anapana. This continued for two full days. I had been telling students to return to

Anapana when any difficulty arises. Now here I was in this predicament.

Normally I find solutions to problems which arise by myself. So what to do? Despite being unable to do Anapana, there was no worry or tension. Sitting quietly, doing nothing, after a few hours on the third day, the resistance cleared and I began working effortlessly with enthusiasm for the remainder of the course.

These experiences have been very helpful for me in learning how to deal with different situations equanimously. May they serve the reader likewise on this path of Dhamma.

—*N. H. Parikh, a retired engineer,*
lives with his wife in Mumbai.

இ

A Rock in the Sea

After twenty-four years practicing Vipassana, I certainly don't feel superior to anyone else. However I do feel that my practice is gently leading my life in a proper direction.

Experiencing the mind and body for the first time as a changing phenomenon was a dramatic event. Practicing equanimity to all that, deep-seated conditioning passed away and the mind felt steam-cleaned and wonderfully calm. Never again has the contrast between the positive and negative been so obvious and consequently the results never so sharply felt.

Successive courses of ten days or more each year have become valued opportunities to work on myself, a time to establish a stronger contact with the deeper levels of being and a chance to let go and link up again with that timeless river of truth flowing within.

Due to my own meditation and direct observation of the laws of cause and effect, I have seen the benefits of avoiding unwholesome actions. My life has become based on the rock of morality which strikes me as a great strength. Surrendering to Dhamma, or truth within, is not a loss. It has enabled me to face important life decisions with the feeling that if I look after Dhamma, Dhamma will look after me. As I have come to understand that only my own reaction to my own sensations can harm me at the ultimate level, I have felt increasingly secure because my happiness has become less dependent on the type of sensation experienced. Consequently I can let things come and go without such deep attachment. Meditation hasn't quite brought with it the "End of History" but it has straightened out many things, making life simpler. Close personal relationships have been completely harmonious and loving. "Ups and downs" have become less because I have led a life more in accordance with natural laws and when they have come, they have ended quicker and been less intense.

Practicing Vipassana brings with it an acutely enhanced awareness of the fleeting nature of life. Thus the beauty of all things is appreciated to a fuller extent and an empathy for things equally ephemeral to myself has grown. At the same time I have been able to live more of my life in the present moment free from the cravings of unfulfilled dreams. Vipassana has shown me how to find completeness and purpose in a swirling sea of change.

—*David Bridges is a schoolteacher in UK.*

Rosebud opens
petal by petal:
Understanding awakens

—*Kathy Henry, USA*

Chapter 7

FREEDOM BEHIND BARS—
VIPASSANA IN PRISONS

We are all prisoners of our own minds . . . Is there anyone who doesn't crave at one point or another to take something that is not his? Is there anyone who doesn't wish, at least once, to hurt the one who hurts him? It is a thin line that separates us from these people, who stare at us from behind bars. The same things that do not go beyond the threshold of our thoughts, have crossed, in their case, the threshold of action. But still, we are alike. Inside our heads we are all potential criminals.

—*Doing Time, Doing Vipassana, Karuna Films*

Jails and prisons are places where criminals are put away. This is their punishment and society is protected by their removal. But when their time is done, what then? If they are not reformed individuals, if their lifelong mental habits are unchanged, the likelihood is they will commit more crimes. Worldwide, treatment programs of all types typically result in recidivism rates of 75% - 80%—about the same as if no rehabilitation is done at all. The public and even many professionals lose enthusiasm for rehabilitation and treatment at times. Crime rates remain high, criminals reoffend, therefore, the argument goes, more prisons are needed. Is there a credible alternative?

Since 1975 Vipassana courses have been conducted in prisons throughout India and in Taiwan, Thailand, Nepal, USA, New Zealand and UK. This unique program is now attracting interest in many countries and offers something that could affect penal systems and treatment programs around the world.

Seattle, USA

The United States incarcerates more people per capita than any country in the world, but will fear of punishment turn criminals into good citizens?

Jail administrator Lucia Meijer agreed to introduce Vipassana into the rehabilitation program after experiencing a course for herself. The North Rehabilitation Facility (NRF) of King County Jail, Seattle, is a minimum security jail for inmates serving short sentences. It houses about 300 men and women whose convictions include robbery, assault, drug dealing and prostitution. As in any jail, severe alcohol and drug problems are common, along with other economic, social and educational disadvantages. There are no cells, walls, guns or lockups. NRF "residents" are kept busy with vocational and/or treatment activities. In a unique, progressive program called "Stages of Change," treatment focuses on drug and alcohol abuse. Other available classes range from Alcoholics Anonymous and Narcotics Anonymous self-help sessions to smoking cessation, critical thinking, parenting and acupuncture. Most residents do take part in the wide range of treatment—but how to break the cycle of reoffending?

For Meijer, Vipassana offers a real opportunity for residents to learn about themselves, take control, and begin to change deep rooted habits of thinking and reacting. With a lifelong experience working in drug and alcohol rehabilitation, she sees Vipassana as an experiential, rather than a spiritually based treatment program:

"Spirituality" is one of those words that functions as a container for any one to fill with their own beliefs and needs. Speaking for myself, we all need a way to face suffering. Suffering includes everything from the knowledge of our own mortality and ultimate aloneness, to the more immediate miseries of each person's life. At NRF, that suffering is pervasive. Inmates here, as everywhere, lose their freedom long before they are incarcerated. Ignorance, abuse, mental illness, addiction, homelessness, poverty, rage, hopelessness, guilt, shame, regret, self-loathing . . . the list is endless.

When an inmate finishes a Vipassana course, he or she has had a glimpse of freedom, perhaps for the first time. Hope and confidence arise from the knowledge that the source and the end of all misery lies within. Because the Vipassana courses designed by S.N. Goenka are taught experientially, this is not just an intellectual exercise but a real encounter with the deepest levels of the mind. Moreover, the inmate has had an experiential lesson in morality. It becomes evident during a course that the ethical base of Vipassana (restraint from killing, stealing, lying, sexual misconduct, and use of intoxicants) are not just rules to be obeyed, but a way for the individual to rise above one's own baser impulses.

The inmate learns that he is his own master and this drastically redefines his or her relationship to authority. Inmates finish a Vipassana course with a much calmer attitude towards institutional rules and constraints. They also come out with a greater capacity to give—usually, the first indication of this is in their expressions of gratitude and a desire to give back to their families and communities.

—Lucia Meijer, NRF Administrator

Inmates have forfeited their freedom; they know first-hand about suffering. The decision to change is theirs alone, no short cuts on the journey inside, no quick fix. It was clear from the start, there would also be no rewards or

incentives for those who volunteered for a Vipassana retreat, nor would they lose anything, such as a job or a
particular residence. Head of Security, Dean Maguire, had
serious doubts ahead of the first course:

> I felt at the time that all the inmates would drop out.
> That they would not participate, that they would not give
> up smoking, their regular meals, their visits, their mail,
> their television, their telephones and their talking for ten
> days. When I was told that, well, I thought. "I don't think
> so!" But "Heck," I said, "go ahead."

To organize a Vipassana course in jail or prison a number of important hurdles have to be cleared. Key staff
members need to be fully informed and committed to the
program to make it work. Since practice is the best way to
understand this technique of meditation, taking a ten-day
course is the ideal preparation. At NRF it was Ben Turner,
a nurse and longtime practitioner of Vipassana, who first
proposed they hold a course. Lucia Meijer and a counsellor from the facility then took their own retreat at the
nearby Washington center and returned convinced. To
maintain noble silence and minimize distractions, prisoners on a course also need to be housed separately from other
non-course inmates. They need their own sleeping accommodation, their own vegetarian diet, their own exercise area.
The solution at NRF was to take over a wing of the jail
normally used for offices or counselling and convert it into
a Vipassana course site complete with meditation room,
dormitories, a dining hall and server areas ready for the
course. Security, requiring twenty compulsory head counts
a day, was a particular concern. Fortunately Ben was a member of the jail personnel and undertook to be course
manager. He was able to take responsibility for head counts
and monitor behavior so that security was not compro-
mised. There were so many potential difficulties—staff had
to move out of their offices, different patterns of work,
security and communication had to be established—but

with goodwill and cooperation of all the NRF staff, the course facilities and schedule were much like those available outside jail.

The first Vipassana course to be held in a North American jail took place in November, 1997. By the third day five of the sixteen men had dropped out, but the remaining eleven completed the ten-day course with remarkable results.

It was like a boot camp for the mind—but you are your own drill sergeant. I felt pain, mental pain. Like a soldier I was going out there on the streets and I was waging a one-man war. Not just with myself, I mean I was waging a war with individuals like yourselves, your children, your daughters, anybody that I came into contact with, the law, I just hated, hated so much . . . .

With everything I experienced in this course, I practically took the sorrow out of myself. For one, my shell of ignorance cracked. I began to see things as they really are right now and not from the past. We do things and we say things but we don't really think about what we do or say. And we don't think about the consequences till afterwards when we're in trouble, and that's a lost cause.

—*Ernest, NRF resident*

Robert Johnson, who had been to jail forty-five times, took a second course after his release, worked as a Vipassana helper and got himself a job as a professional cook. His example and achievement had a powerful impact on fellow inmates and family. His mother, a devoutly Christian woman, was so thrilled with changes she saw in him that she took a course too.

Three years on, enjoying regular life outside jail, Robert reflects:

When you're in an addiction you don't know it. That's
the problem. You can't stop the cycle so usually someone
has to stop you and then you will probably hate that
person because you think you're doing the right thing.
So I was in an addiction. I wouldn't be able to stop myself.
The way I'd slow down was by getting arrested by the
police, being in some hideous fight, or a car accident. It
would take something like that to stop me. If I had any
sense you'd think I'd realize, "If I hadn't been doing drugs
and all that stuff, I wouldn't find myself in this type of
trouble." That's if I could take an honest look at myself,
but I didn't know too much about honesty in those days
. . . 'cause if I'd been honest, I wouldn't have taken the
first drink. "You can just do it one more time," I always
thought. But I was just lying to myself. . . .

Robert's family was a mix of schoolteachers and min-
isters as well as criminals. A promising student, he had a
dream to become a pilot. But the neighborhood was full of
addicts, pot smokers, cocaine users and he found himself
drawn to those out for a party, staying up nights high as a
kite while trying to study. All his life he'd wanted to go to
university but it didn't pan out. Somehow everything got
mixed up with drink and drugs. Scared off flying by in-
structors' warnings and the doped-up antics of a fellow
trainee, he quit the course. Next year he enrolled at a college in Texas, away from the home crowd. The opening
was there, and nowhere left for him to run.

It all starts when something very subtle happens inside.
I can tell you now what it was, but back then I didn't
know. The fact is I got restless. So, in an attempt to pass
my time, I'd take off down the street and when I drank
some alcohol that just made it that much worse because
whatever I'm thinking, I'm doing. Each time I got angry
or my mental state wasn't too wholesome, whatever
thought popped into my mind—I would do it. For years
I'd gone past one particular store wondering why it had
never been broken into. And again, that day after my dad
died, it popped into my head. It seemed right then,

everything was going wrong—drinking, nothing to do, angry, Dad died suddenly. I was terribly upset. So, very drunk, I cleaned the place out. Loaded it all into my truck early that morning, not knowing the police were over the street looking. They let me take everything from the store, then blocked the street and pulled me over. "Where're you going, Mr Johnson?" they smiled. I woke up in a jail cell . . . .

Robert kept bouncing back to jail. Out one month, back the next. So far into the jailhouse scene, it meant nothing to him. Eight months was the longest he stayed out over a ten year period.

There were fights, disruptive behavior, driving charges, violations of home detention—each one adding to my record. Every time I broke the law was serious, it destroyed my life. Once you get into the cycle of going into jail and coming out, you hit the floor so often eventually you don't bother to get up, 'cause it's only a matter of time before you're in jail again. Whatever it is you've accomplished, when you go into jail you lose most if not all of it because you get cut off from your friends, your family, job, your support . . . .

Robert took all the therapeutic programs but nothing worked. He even went to church twice a day for a while until something inside erupted and tore it all apart again. Then he saw a notice about Vipassana on the bulletin board, a way to break the jail cycle.

Can I try? I was desperate going into that course, didn't know anything about meditation. I was mad at the jail staff, they gave us all these classes but nobody ever talked about how things change. So I just forgot those plans for the day written on my mirror. I never had the peace I needed when those other feelings came up and I'd land back in jail.

So he sat in that first Vipassana retreat and gave himself a big surprise.

What I got out of that course is something no one else was ever able to give me. Actually it wasn't anything anybody gave me, so nobody can take it away.

It's strange. At the very root of it, something way down deep happened, whereby whatever it is I'm doing I never do it the same way I did in the past. If I get angry it's a different type of anger, less and with no big reaction. Since that first course, I slowed down enough to think about something before I do it. Before, I just wouldn't. Consequently by just doing those things and trying to keep the five precepts, I never went back to jail, never seen a policeman. That's a big change, right there. After that course I just don't react the same—something happened.

—*Robert Johnson, NRF resident*

Spurred on by the early response, more courses were arranged at NRF, for women as well as men. With some infrastructure already in place and building on experience, it proved easier for residents, staff and Vipassana volunteers to set up a temporary meditation center in the jail's counselling wing and run the courses.

Right before I came in, I was in a really bad way . . . a heroin addict and pretty close to death. It was bad. And I was tired of that and I kicked and that was hell. I knew if I went back out there, I might not make it very much longer. So I knew I had to do something. And when I was chosen to go to the Vipassana (post-course) graduation ceremony for the men, I couldn't believe the change that I had seen . . . From that moment I knew I wanted to do this.

—*Susan, NRF resident*

The women find the course no less difficult than the men. Each one fighting her own separate battle. At times the challenge of remaining detached and balanced despite the intensity of the experience seems overwhelming. Shelia went to a helper, feeling unwell and on the verge of giving up.

So I gave it one more hour. Then later on, Lucia came and I grabbed her hand and I said, "I can't do it, I just can't do it." And Lucia said, "I know how you feel, 'cause during my course I packed my bags also and was ready to go. And then something stopped me." And she talked me into staying. And I'm glad that I did stay and complete the course.

—Shelia, NRF resident

From their viewpoint, prison staff witnessed immediate effects in the inmate meditators:

I saw honesty. I saw these residents being honest about themselves and not lying to themselves anymore. I saw them being very open and not bothered by the rules. The security staff was here for a reason; the rules were here for a reason. That was what made me see there was some real change there. Because some of those people were behavior problems before they went into meditation. They weren't when they came out.

—Dean Maguire, Head of Security

Almost to a man, there was something behind their eyes— you couldn't get in. There was like this curtain hanging. Then when the course was over, you could see inside. I can't say what the course did for each one of them for the rest of their lives, but in ten days you could see inside them. They were there. You could see they were there. Whereas before, they weren't there. You couldn't see them. And I think that's really exciting . . . .

—Stephanie Maxwell, Program Director

I came to Vipassana not as a seeker but by accident. Now I've seen the benefits of meditation personally, at home and in my working life. I try to keep improving, sitting daily, taking retreats when I can. Still I recidivate all the time, losing my temper, cheating here and there . . . When it comes to jail, do we seriously expect people with lifetimes of serious pathology to always be upstanding and fully productive citizens from now on? At NRF we're not looking for some "magic bullet" solution. We aim to work incrementally with each person on an authentic and subtle level to produce real, sustainable changes in their behavior. When it comes to judging the effect of Vipassana on an individual, we take a realistic view of what is meant by "success." Who has volunteered to work on themselves in this way, what it takes in courage and commitment to get them through the course, after effects—the way they act in jail—and finally, when they leave, do we see them back again?

—Lucia Meijer, NRF Administrator

Residents themselves felt different after the course: I love myself today. I do . . . it's a wonderful feeling. And these tears are tears of happiness, they truly are. I was really kind of fearful . . . things I've been running from all my life. And it was right there in my face and I really just had to look at it—observe, and let go. I was able to do that. And there's such a peace and such a weight lifted, I can't tell you.

—Susan, NRF resident

I learned to work with the sensations inside. If there's some tense situation, like a confrontation in the dorm, I can be really aware of how I'm feeling and what's going on inside. So when I get into those situations on the outside, I know it'll all pass.

—Carol, NRF resident

Vipassana is progressive along a sometimes uneven path of transformation. Although dramatic changes can and do occur, so can setbacks. So much depends on the individual. At NRF however, staff have seen enough to be optimistic—and extend the program. Vipassana "residents" are encouraged to maintain their meditation, group sittings are regularly held in the jail and as more courses are held, they can give support by sitting as old students or giving service in the kitchen.

If it were just a matter of effort and desire, they would all be better . . . They didn't have a way. And Vipassana gave them a way. It gave them a tool. It gave them a choice. Now I'm not for a minute saying that they will always make the right choice from now on. But they have a choice now, and they didn't have one before.

—*Lucia Meijer, NRF Administrator*

&

Vipassana changed my relationships, how I would talk, react, function around people, that's what the meditation did. I'm not a slave of my mind anymore. I can choose not to think negatively about a person. I can choose to think very positively about them. Vipassana gave me these type of tools, it makes you feel better, makes you act better. Some people don't have a choice in the matter. What they feel, they have to obey. But I don't have that anymore.

—*Robert Johnson, former NRF resident*

Lancaster, UK

"I knew it was going to happen, It's needed so badly. There's an amazing amount of potential inside prisons." Twenty years on since he did time himself, Darren Bowman went back to jail voluntarily as a helper on a Vipassana course at

Lancaster Castle Prison in 1998. He'd grown up a rebel, getting tough with anything that crossed him—bosses, the law—until the inevitable happened and he was sent down. But inside this violent, angry person was someone looking for more—for sincerity and decency. Darren became friends with a woman who was everything he wasn't but yet put no pressure on him. She became sick with leukemia and he nursed her back to health. Sadly she relapsed while he was in prison and died. The shock was enough to start him turning his life around. Once out of prison, by chance, he took a Vipassana course. He bridled at the rules, desperate to run, but something kept him going to the end. The next year was one of turmoil; he kept denying any good came of his meditation. Friends, however, kept saying how different he'd become. When Darren sat his second course he stopped fighting with himself and took the practice on board. He saw now that, one hundred per cent, this was what he'd been looking for. When the opportunity arose to serve a course in prison he volunteered right away.

> I knew within five minutes of meeting those inmates that we were on the same wavelength. All my street life, all my time in prison was going to be of value. "You had to do that, Darren, to do this." I never felt so focused as in those ten days.
>
> —*Darren Bowman, UK*

Lancaster is a medium security prison located in the center of this northern city, within the original castle walls. It holds about 215 male prisoners, serving sentences from several months to life. Paul Thompson, the governor, had heard about the positive impact of Vipassana in Indian and U.S. jails and was keen to host a course as a pilot project. The prison already ran classes on drug rehabilitation and anger management but this ten-day intensive experience would be the first of its kind in Europe.

Two officers, Chris Berry and Paul Bevan, had sat Vipassana courses and they took on responsibility for arrangements within the prison. They put up posters about the upcoming event and spoke to inmates about the technique. Prisoners knew these officers well from previous programs and trusted them. Over a period of weeks, meditator volunteers visited the jail to meet interested inmates, show film of earlier prison courses and answer questions. A small self-contained area where prisoners and course workers could be accommodated with least disturbance was prepared.

Eight men committed themselves to attend the course, nearly all had spent many terms in jail. Familiar problems soon surfaced—occasional talking between the students and furtive smoking. Keeping to a discipline that's stricter than prison discipline without being forced is tough. After a few days a leader in the group came clean, saying they'd do their best in future to stick to course rules. They followed the timetable well and meditated seriously. As the course progressed, the mood began to change. One night a veteran warder who had just finished locking up other rowdy prisoners was astounded to see the meditator group walk silently to their cells. "What have you done to them!" he exclaimed and then started asking questions. Next morning he told a volunteer he'd been trying to observe his own breath during the shift. Officers who had previously been cynical began to show a genuine interest. But in the sweepstake they'd organized no one bet on all eight completing the course—and that was the outcome.

A press photographer came to take some shots of the men meditating. One inmate asked him if he wanted to know what Vipassana was.

"Yes," the photographer replied.

"OK," said Jamie. "Give me your camera."

The photographer gave him the camera.

"Now turn around."

The photographer turned around.

"Now turn back," said Jamie.

The photographer turned back.

"Here's your camera," said Jamie. "Before Vipassana I would have been out the door with it, but now, after Vipassana, here it is!"

On the final morning, participants, their families and staff gathered to mark what had been accomplished.

As the course went on, I felt myself changing. I was getting happier about myself and stronger in my conviction to stay off drugs. I was gaining confidence in myself and as I let go of the fears and ill-will I'd bottled up inside, I felt love flow in its place . . . This course allowed me to blow away the black clouds in my head and forgive myself, in part at least, for the misery I've caused. I don't expect anyone who has been a victim of my past to forgive me as easily, but maybe as they see a change in me, they'll at least accept I'm no longer that person.

—*Hugh, Lancaster inmate*

Darren, onetime convict turned marine fitter and volunteer helper, summed it up:

They are learning they have to do it for themselves. They've plenty of determination, had to have that to survive, that's why they came through the course. Before they had nothing. With Vipassana what they've now got is hope.

New Delhi, India

Tihar Jail is India's best known high security prison. With an inmate population of over 10,000, it is one of the largest prisons in the world. For decades Tihar was notorious for its inhuman conditions. A hellish, violent, congested coop where corruption was rife and the regime punitively harsh. However a breakthrough came to Tihar with the appointment of Kiran Bedi, India's first woman police officer, to head the jail in 1993. Bedi had a vision of prison as a place for personal development and systematically set about broadening staff perceptions of their role—from guards to guardians, educators, reformists. And rapid-fire action followed.

We kept using a lot of love and care, actually giving the prisoners love and care. I allowed them books, canteen facilities, better medical care, clothing, radio, outside visitors . . . .

—*Kiran Bedi, Inspector General, Tihar Jail*

Mustafa, a foreign inmate from Africa, comments: Before she came the most devilish, evil things used to happen in this jail. It was a really horrible place. Ever since she took office, she did a lot of transformation. Before we were regarded here as, I don't know really, it's beyond description. With sincerity, with a compassionate heart, she showed us that we are human beings. Therefore we deserve to be treated as human beings.

The atmosphere in Tihar improved but Bedi was seeking a deeper change. Many inmates wanted to change themselves but lacked the skills to handle their problems. How to give them these skills, the positive qualities the human mind needs? Unexpectedly the answer came from a young officer at the prison, Rajinder Kumar, who recounted to Bedi his own experience with Vipassana meditation.

I was a very angry man. I would be horrible as a person but I went for Vipassana and now I'm a different person. Madam, if you don't believe me, ask my family, ask my colleagues. If you introduce this course in jail, it will help all the inmates.

In fact this technique had previously been tried in Indian prisons. In Jaipur in 1975 prisoners learned Vipassana for the first time. The authorities relaxed their rules to permit the teacher to stay in the jail during the course and even allowed chains to be removed from dangerous prisoners despite the security risk. The Jaipur experiment concluded peacefully and its success led to more courses in other prisons. At Baroda the superintendent of the jail was impressed by the effect of Vipassana on his prisoners and decided to take a course himself.

The coordination between prisoners and staff has improved. Relationships between prisoners and their families have also improved. Prisoners' thoughts of revenge, "After I get out of here, I'll kill this person, I'll do this and that . . .," all have been wiped out.

—*R.L. Vora, Prison Administrator, Baroda, India*

Babu Bhaya was convicted for killing three people in five minutes during a gang fight. After a Vipassana course at Baroda Jail, he was so filled with remorse that he pleaded forgiveness from his victims' families.

They agreed to put the past behind us, and on the day of the "Rakhi" festival those two women came and tied a sacred thread on my wrist, taking me as their foster brother. Today I look after their family as if it was my own.

Bedi prepared the ground for a Vipassana course at Tihar, sending some members of her staff to attend a retreat outside the jail and inviting prisoners to participate. Over one hundred inmates and jail staff took part in the jail's first course in November 1993. Kiran Bedi and her

team were delighted. They had found a remedy, there was no looking back. In the following year an ambitious course serving over one thousand inmates was given within the jail and a permanent meditation center was established in one of the cell blocks.
It actually changed people. It made my prisoners weep. It made them cry. They had realized what life actually could be. They had looked within. And within themselves they had seen the feelings of revenge, they had seen anger, they saw the disrespect and hurt they had caused to family and society, and they wept. And they wanted to be different.

—*Kiran Bedi, Inspector General, Tihar Jail*

Kiran Bedi was transferred from Tihar in 1995, but thanks to her efforts and those of her colleagues and successors, the Vipassana program continues to flourish. Two ten-day courses a month are held at the jail center, with volunteer workers serving their fellow prisoners. The process of transformation in individuals and the institution is continuing.

❧

Change does not come the easy way. Change takes time. I'm not telling you I did a Vipassana course and bam! anger, my quick temper, completely went out at one time. It's still subsiding, subsiding, subsiding.

—*Mustafa, Tihar inmate*

A new benchmark in prison reform was set in Summer 1999 when the first twenty-day course for senior meditator inmates was conducted at the Tihar Jail center. Serious long courses of meditation are periodically given at established centers to enable suitably qualified students to purify their minds at deeper levels and progress more rapidly. With the full cooperation of the jail authorities, this was the first long Vipassana retreat to be held inside prison walls. Fifteen inmates took part, each with his own separate living and meditation space. The course was marked by perfect discipline, timekeeping and noble silence; so much so that even prison staff were amazed at the kind of environment that prevailed in the jail center during those three whole weeks. Following a feedback session with inmates after the course, one senior official said he felt he'd been at a temple for an hour listening to spiritual discussions rather than meeting prisoners in jail—and promised to sit a course himself at the earliest opportunity.

Kiran Bedi meanwhile moved on to being a Police Commissioner in Delhi, sat her own first Vipassana course and organized another huge ten-day retreat for twelve hundred police personnel in the Delhi Police Training College in March 1999.

A technique which is effective here will be definitely effective anywhere in the world. Prisons in the West, prisons in the East, man in the West, man in the East— no difference! Difference of degree, but in totality we are the same.

—Ram Singh, Vipassana Teacher

Unlocking Doors

Compassionate discipline within the correctional system is our best hope. Vipassana will not cure the problem of crime but it will orient us in the right direction. Vipassana represents all that is needed—discipline, self-control, morality, compassion and a keen understanding of the law of cause and effect.

—Lucia Meijer, U.S. Jail Administrator

I recommend that Vipassana meditation be available to every prisoner in the system, male and female. No one can undertake it without getting something from the experience. An individual has got to want to do it, it's not easy! However the rewards are very great. I know there are people like me in the system who want and need help. They are sick of the cycle of drinking, drugs, violence and crime, but it's been part of their lives for so long that they just can't see a way out of it. Vipassana can give them a different direction. Inner leadership so to speak. And Vipassana costs nothing! Just think how much money it will save the tax man over the coming years if the technique can help inmates like me to be calmer and more focused on a positive future, both during our sentence and after release.

—Brian Worthing, Lancaster inmate

Results from a simple recidivism study of the first eight courses held at NRF, the Seattle jail, show that two years after the completion of at least one Vipassana course residents are rebooked about half as often as they had been in the two years prior to their course (from 2.9 bookings, on average, to 1.5 bookings). The over all return rate of NRF residents to the King County Jail system within two years of release is 75%. For those who have done a Vipassana course, the return rate after two years is 56%.

Orientation classes held in the few weeks before a retreat have helped intending students understand the Vipassana ground rules and prepare for the course. Completion rates have risen as a consequence and inmates now meditate more effectively. In recognition of progress made, the U.S. National Institute of Health has funded a two year detailed study by a team from the University of Washington to evaluate the impact of Vipassana on alcohol/drug use and other behavioral changes among inmates. Meanwhile early in 2001 after two and a half year's preparatory work with the Sheriff of San Francisco and local jail staff, an inmate course was held at San Bruno, one of this beacon city's own jails, with more to follow. In 2002 two Vipassana courses were held at the Donaldson Maximum Security Prison outside Birmingham, Alabama, with dramatic early results that will no doubt be the source of much more research and documentation as time goes on.

Research by the All India Institute of Medical Sciences and others has shown that successful completion of a Vipassana meditation course increases inmates' awareness of their emotions, resulting in a reduction in feelings of anger, tension, hostility, revenge and hopelessness. Drug addiction, neurotic and psychopathological symptoms are also diminished. As a result of the measurable gains recorded, the Indian Government recommended that Vipassana courses be held in jails throughout the country. To date, ten-day retreats are being conducted regularly at more than fifteen prisons in India.

Vipassana has also been successfully used within a special prison program in New Zealand. The Te Ihi Tu Trust is a Government backed "habilitation" center run by Maori, the indigenous people of the islands, for Maori prerelease inmates. It is the only center in the country specifically designed for Maori and embracing "kaupapa," Maori values, culture and thinking in a holistic way. Vipassana came to be included in this challenging program for parolees as a result of the influence of staff member Marua Wharepouri. After completing his own first ten-day course he was convinced that the technique would help residents make the necessary changes in their lives. Together with another staff member who had taken a course some years earlier, preparations were made to hold a course at the Te Ihi Tu Trust premises. The site was formerly a wing of New Plymouth hospital and has traditional significance for local Maori people. Staff at Te Ihi Tu responded with real enthusiasm and confidence and the first course passed off smoothly, with no sense of conflict between the practice of Vipassana and the Maori way of life. They had received a "taonga" or treasure, one student commented. Further courses have taken place since.

All kinds of doors have been opened for us, residents and staff alike. It is no more "us and them," there is no prison culture here. There is only we and we are Maori, strong in our beliefs and culture . . . I'm proud of the men!

—*Te Wai, staff member*

Vipassana helped me get over a lot of issues that I feel have been holding me back.

—*Te Ara Puanga, former resident,*
now released and in work

I live in a society where people share the same problems of many indigenous people all over the world, poverty, lost language and identity, colonization and poor education systems. As also throughout the world with indigenous people, young Maori men are disproportionately populating the prisons in New Zealand. I, for one, am a result of this.

So you can expect the type of individual I am and I won't go into the details of my life experiences however terrible they may have been. But this disturbing existence caused me to live in my head and withdraw from society. Simply, I was unable to function successfully without harming others and eventually deteriorating to the point of harming myself out of confusion, frustration and desperation.

Receiving a substantial prison sentence caused me to evaluate myself for my own benefit and for the wellbeing of my two lovely young children. This is what opened my eyes and made me reach out to the Te Ihi Tu Trust and the challenge of learning Vipassana meditation within the habilitation program; three months of continuous practice and continuous change which brought me relief, self control and a toehold on a more wholesome lifestyle. Now I know I too can change, it's the law of nature.

—*Tau Hae Ngaru, Te Ihi Tu resident*

Chapter 8

THE COMPASS—VIPASSANA AND THE YOUNG

Grown ups think that children don't have problems, but we do . . . missing my mum, worrying about school work, feeling lonely, getting angry with my little sister. Why do I get so upset? Can't I stop being bad tempered? So often I don't get what I want, I feel terrible and I hate everybody! I don't want to be like this!

—The Path of Joy, *Veronica Logan,*
Vipassana Research Publications

Childhood is a time of discovery. Every moment can bring a new experience. Every day can be an exploration into the unknown, full of promise and of danger. It's a time to start learning about life and how to live it. But for children today, learning about life is harder than ever before; the world is changing so rapidly. All too easily they may feel confused or uncertain; all too often they may lose their sense of direction. There is a compass children can learn to use, and with it they can find their way through life. That compass is called Vipassana meditation.

—The Compass, *Karuna Films*

Custom Courses

Short courses designed especially for children and young people are given in many of the Vipassana centers in Western and Asian countries. Courses for children vary in length from one to three days according to their age, the seriousness of the course and location. Youngsters are taught in two age groupings, 8 to 12 or 13 to 16, and generally stay over at the center for the two and three day events.

Children come to learn meditation with many of the same aims and hopes as adults. Some hope "to become nicer to be around." Others wish to be able to deal with stressful situations or to become more self-confident. Some may know about meditation from their parents or friends, for others it's an entirely new experience.

On these short courses Anapana meditation, the preparatory step for learning Vipassana, is taught to the children. Periods of Anapana and counselling are alternated with physical and creative activities, which are linked to themes related to the meditation.

The course starts with a short meeting where the adult helpers introduce themselves and explain the layout of the center, the schedule and the basic rules the youngsters will be expected to follow.

The children then enter the meditation hall where they meet the teachers and receive beginning instructions. First they promise to follow a code of moral conduct during the time they are at the center—that is, to avoid any words or actions that would harm others and make their own minds agitated. This is a key part of the technique; it helps the children become calm and quiet enough to be able to look within.

Next they start meditating by learning the technique of Anapana—awareness of breath, to focus and calm the mind. The children are asked to close their eyes and try to remain aware of the natural breath entering and leaving the nostrils. Simple as the exercise is, it can be surprisingly hard: the mind keeps slipping away to memories, fantasies, fears, hopes or sometimes to sleep.

When they told me about what meditation was and the reason why people do it, I think that helped me a lot and the first time we meditated I tried as hard as I could because I knew that I would benefit from it.

—*Carla, age 13*

For a birthday treat my friends were going abseiling, and here I was missing it!

—*Meredith, age 13*

On Friday afternoon I noticed that it was raining and I found the meditation difficult because of school. I could hear things that people had said because usually on a Friday everyone's hyper and it was a bit of a rush getting to the center. On Saturday morning the birds were singing and I could do the meditation quite easily.

—*Peter, age 13*

The task is to keep bringing the mind back to the chosen object until gradually it starts to stay, to become concentrated. Naturally this doesn't happen all at once; it takes time and effort.

Breath coming in, going out, coming in, going out... suddenly I realized that all the monkeys in my mind had stopped wandering... I think I am starting to become master of my mind and I feel so peaceful.

—The Path of Joy, *Veronica Logan*

The children meditate for periods up to half an hour at a time. Afterwards they divide up into groups and discuss their experiences, with a counsellor on hand to answer questions, clear up confusions and give guidance.

Okay, so you're in the dinner queue. There are only two baked potatoes left and you're quite hungry but somebody else is behind you. What are you going to do?

The busy timetable includes breaks and rest periods. On the schedule are games, physical exercises, storytelling and various creative activities. On one course the group designed and made their own meditation cushions, on another they painted lifesize portraits of themselves to be displayed with helpful signs for the center's open house next day.

As time goes by, the children fall into the rhythm of the course. They enjoy the activities, get to know each other, and start to appreciate the meditation sessions.

I don't know about you, but I feel much better after that!

Keeping the promises outside is hard, watching your language, not doing harm when you've been hurt. And what do you do if friends get into a fight?..

Talking through the experiences really helps and makes the actual meditation easier . . . .

—*Postcourse feedback from young people, UK, 1998*

They also begin to understand the purpose of what they are doing. The mind, they are told, is a jumble of positive and negative qualities—and they can see it for themselves in the play of thoughts that tug at them as they meditate. When they successfully keep attention on the breath, on the reality of the present moment, negative thoughts fade away and positivity remains. The awareness of breath becomes their best friend, always on hand to help them in difficulties.

When I arrived I was especially worried about school because a lot of homework was piled on me at the last minute. But even though it still bothers me now, I am much more relaxed and I have put it more into perspective. Instead of stressing I am trying to think of ways to do it quickly and work more efficiently. This weekend has also made me realize how I sometimes judge people negatively, when in fact I don't know them. I'll try harder from now on to give everyone a fair chance before deciding what they are like.

—Petra, age 16

My meditation has gone well, it becomes easier and more natural with practice. I would like to become more attentive to everything around me, especially people, and to be more alert and observant. Also I'd like to be more forgiving, I find it hard to mend a relationship after becoming enemies. Apart from the meditation, what I really like about the center is the environment, atmosphere and people. When I'm here I feel very far away from my problems, there's never any bitchiness and it's very trusting—everyone's nice, no one steals, you don't have to lock your room . . . .

—Kim, age 16

I am always impressed at the effort they put in; they really persevere at their meditation. Normally if children don't like what they are doing, they drop it and move on to something else. But here, despite hitches, they keep coming back to the breath. That's such a refreshing change and they gain something of real value by doing it. The courses are a wonderful opportunity to work with some young people who are interested in beginning a spiritual journey, who are ready to listen and take on something new.

—*Reinette Brown is a children's course teacher.*
She works in an English primary school
teaching an Early Years class.

Mindful Schooling

The technique of Anapana is not being taught only in Vipassana centers. Schools also have been requesting courses and making time for children to meditate during the working day. Why?

Around the world, modern education tends to emphasize intellectual growth and academic results over other aspects of a person's development. The emotional and spiritual dimensions, so important in building individual character, are frequently eclipsed or neglected. Parents and schools realize that something is lacking but most do not know how to help children grow at the inner level. Anapana meditation is a solution to this. By developing self awareness through observation of the breath, young people from primary school age on can learn to look inside themselves and get in touch with their own needs. The ability to live in the present with a balanced mind fosters a positive attitude and outlook. Through their own direct experience children learn a simple, straightforward and logical message that by not harming others through their mental, vocal and physical actions, they actually help themselves and those around them.

India is a secular country, where state schools are not allowed to teach any particular religion. Anapana courses have been welcomed by many schools as a way of introducing a learning method which focuses on the child's total development and is universally acceptable and free from controversy. Inculcating humane values is at the heart of education but teaching morality to the younger generation is difficult and may even be counterproductive unless an effective technique is available to train the mind. Courses of Anapana cover both these aspects.

There are some schools where Anapana meditation has been introduced as part of the curriculum, providing one practice period of half an hour daily. In other places, the entire school practices daily for five to ten minutes and each year refresher courses are held. School teachers are asked to participate in the courses along with the students so that they can lead by example and become partners in this constructive activity. Children are wary of preaching; they don't like sermons but when they see their teacher engaged in the same work he or she is asking them to do, they respond easily and eagerly.

I like to meditate because it is helping me a lot after just a two-day course. I am going to practice it and not give up. I was very happy learning that every morning we will meditate in school.

—*Mohammed, age 13*

Concentrating on your breath takes not much effort, because we're concentrating on something we already have, and something which is very easy to concentrate on. Of course at first you do feel restless but later on it becomes quite effortless.

—*Rajesh, age 16*

It happened once that I fought with one of my friends, and I was going to shout at her but no, I thought, I can't do that. So I just concentrated on my breath for about a minute or so, and then it just came back to normal . . . I didn't shout.

—*Nassim, age 16*

The meditation course was definitely a very positive step towards self-betterment. As adults we have also learned a lot and I already feel the changes in me to tackle life with a more proactive approach and this can only improve with regular meditation. It also brought peace of mind and I earnestly feel that it should be part of the school curriculum.

—Manju Rajan is a class teacher at Gitanjali
Senior School, Hyderabad, India.

Questionnaires sent to parents and class teachers confirm the impact of the courses on youngsters' behavior. Negative qualities like quarrelsomeness, abusive language, being disruptive in class and various complexes decrease. Simultaneously positive qualities such as honesty, helpfulness and self confidence increase. The academic performance of those who continue to meditate at home or at school also improves because the meditation helps to enhance concentration and memory.

In this way thousands of young people in India are experiencing the advantages of Anapana meditation, not only in mainstream schools but also in specialized settings such as at correctional facilities, orphanages, rehabilitation homes and schools for the blind and for children with other disabilities.

Initial contacts have also been made with schools in Australia, North America and Europe, as a result of which small numbers of children have started practicing Anapana. In Germany, one school sent a whole class to the center for a residential three-day course. In the USA an Anapana program was organized at a summer camp in Washington and in California children are invited to join a course at the local Vipassana center.

Karen Donovan, a schoolteacher and children's course teacher in the U.S., recalls how the technique helped one young boy in an unexpected emergency:

A couple of years ago Andrew, one of our students who attended a children's course, fell ill during our end of the year class campout. The week after we returned, he was hospitalized and nearly died as a result of a severe allergic reaction to some drugs he was given for his illness. His entire body, inside and out, swelled and blistered. The doctors thought he would be blind and have brain damage if he survived, and his chances were slim for survival. His older brother Casey (our former student) who had also come to the children's course, kept a vigil by his side with their mother, Katherine, who has not sat a course. Katherine later told us that Casey kept reminding Andrew to observe his breath and practice Anapana whenever he came to consciousness. He knew what excruciating pain Andrew was in and he thought that it might help him deal with it. Andrew said he did use Anapana during his time in the hospital and that it helped with the pain as well as with the boredom he experienced through the long weeks of recovery.

Andrew did recover fully and regained his sight completely. The following year, when the children's course came around again, they both attended and practiced very seriously. Andrew, who has a pattern of teasing other children, told me that he was hoping that Anapana would help him break that habit because he knows when he does it, it hurts others' feelings and is wrong. He said, "I need to gain control of my mind so I can stop myself from doing it."

In the West today even the preteens are increasingly sophisticated, image conscious, prone to peer pressure and consider themselves more like young adults than children. Although most are not brought up with a strong religious identity, they may be spiritually inclined. They are questioning and curious but are turned off by being told this is the way it is. They are socially and environmentally aware, have a sense of justice and the ability to reason intellectually on moral issues. They respond to an invitation to look inside and discover for themselves what reality is. They are interested in unlocking the mind's secrets. Learning Anapana helps bridge the gap between intellectual understanding and the ability to act accordingly. For parents too it provides an opportunity for genuine spiritual instruction, free from religious pronouncements.

ॐ

Olwen: Courses help them to understand the foundation, the moral code, and you do try to put it into practice, don't you. Like it wouldn't come easy for you to take something off someone else, you wouldn't see the point . . . .

Stephanie: When you know the five "promises," you try to not break them as much, like hurting people's feelings, trying not to lie or deliberately standing on an insect . . . .

Steve: That in itself is a tremendous achievement, because, although she does Religious Education, it means nothing really. It's a subject at school taught in its own peculiar way and with its own particular dogma and goals. Kids just want to get their exams, the next step on the educational ladder. It doesn't really mean anything.

—Olwen is a horticultural worker, Steve is a nurse and Stephanie age 15 studies at the local high school. In conversation, the Smith family from Liverpool, UK.

ॐ

Lorraine Mitchell has worked as a helper on courses in India as well as in her native Australia:

As an educator and a carer, I am asked not to pressure children in any particular direction too much, to leave all choices open to the individual. It is unfortunate that this has lead to a kind of paralysis on the part of guardians of our children's education and an overwhelming sense of burden on our youth. As young pliable minds, they are asking us to teach them how to close the doors to experiences which could harm themselves or others. Guiding children to find harmony cannot be dangerous. Rather it is our human obligation to encourage young people to strive to live a harmonious and beneficial life.

🐚

The difference a course makes can even take their teacher by surprise:

The contrast was truly remarkable. This same class of twenty-three teenage rowdies who had earlier put everyone on the train through torture, now chatting quietly on the way home, offering their seats, being complimented by other passengers . . . .

—Peter Baumann teaches secondary school students in southern Germany. He and his wife Anita are also children's course teachers.

Wise Heads on Young Shoulders

After a course, parents and teachers are hopeful that youngsters will continue to practice Anapana regularly at home. In some cases this does happen but more often they return to meditation from time to time in response to particular situations or needs.

What the experience of meditation has given anyone cannot easily be measured. It may just sow a good seed or nourish a sapling. It may encourage someone to take a full Vipassana course when they feel ready, to learn how to purify the mind at a deeper level. This is like completing the job, adding a roof to the floor and walls of their meditation cabin.

I first learned about this type of meditation from my aunt when I was nine years old. Since then I've come to many children's courses. Meditation has certainly affected the ways in which I approach life. I have learned to face situations where there is anger or frustration and say to myself "Be calm, breathe!" This type of attitude is in contrast to many of my friends and I hope they take notice of my responses and learn from them . . . The courses have been wonderful as I've met lots of new people, young and old, and enjoyed the countryside (something I don't see everyday in the city). I do find, however, that meditation is more difficult at home as neither of my parents do it. I try to meditate every other day and in situations of stress, like exams. By returning to the center for these courses I learn more and can therefore progress in my practice. I hope soon I will be able to complete a ten-day course and after university visit India and perhaps do a course there . . . .

—*Tracey Shipton, age 17, lives in London,
working for a website company in her
gap year before starting college.*

With parents' agreement, a young person can take a Vipassana course from the age of sixteen. Sarah Brightwell from Australia, who joined her first retreat at the exceptional age of ten, recalls a turning point:

That day was probably the best day of the course. I was full of anger, meanness, unkindness and wouldn't do anything I didn't want to do and showed it all immensely. But late that same night I realized that that was the day that all my negativities didn't like me any more and decided to go to someone else, and then I suddenly felt happy.

Kim Burgess, now at university, also took a ten-day course before her teens and has been practicing ever since:

It is difficult for me to imagine how different my life might have been without this tool of Vipassana, as it has simply been an integral part of my life. Yet from an early age I remember looking for a point to life; wondering why we were here amidst so much misery; why joy was so shortlived. Vipassana provided the answers . . . It has given me a deep inner security and a selfdependence, with the realization that I can't blame anything on anyone else, but that I'm solely responsible for the future.

For Kamala Gedam, a girl of 17 in southern India, Vipassana helps ease troubled times:

I used to pass through phases of depression (though for no obvious reason) and periods when I would grow rebellious. I still do sometimes, like most teenagers. But now I see that I don't waste as much time brooding or feeling lethargic as I used to. My outlook towards my student life has also changed. Known for my rebellious nature, I have certainly calmed down and become more optimistic.

The practice of meditation will always help someone grow in Dhamma but it may not be for everyone. A loving, respectful and supportive family environment enables youngsters to make their own wise choices.

I've never felt that the goal of Stephanie's youth is to learn how to meditate. I've always felt that meditation is part and parcel of her Dhamma, a wholesome way of life. And every aspect of Stephanie's life is inundated with Dhamma because of us. The parents have such an important influence on a child that if we're doing it properly she'll pick up so much that's positive that when she's able to choose for herself what style of life to lead, she's got every possibility of making an informed decision and a good choice. I just want her to see that in Vipassana there's something which we find tremendously valuable,

the most important thing in our lives, and that she's
allowed to grow up as normal as possible . . . .
We're honest with her. We're not playing any games.
She knows that we want her to be her own person and
we're trying to help her.

She's really got to come to it with her own free will, in
her own time, and it might not necessarily be to meditate.

—*In conversation, the Smith family,*
Liverpool, UK

❧

Toddlers to teenagers, parents also find they have plenty
to learn from having children in the family.

Being a parent is probably one of the most difficult and
delicate jobs in our society. It requires infinite patience.
To be a truly good parent you must have infinite love
with total detachment. Aren't these the qualities Dhamma
teaches us? The arrival of your child is a perfect test for
whether you have really cultivated these qualities in
yourself through your meditation. First come those
sleepless nights after your baby's birth. When my
daughter was born, for weeks I used to sleep three hours
and sit two hours a day. Then come the tantrums, not to
talk of the constant demands and total deprivation of any
kind of freedom whatsoever. But worst of all is the
attachment, the strong attachment you develop for your
child . . . You have to watch yourself very carefully. See
how many parents spoil or even destroy their children
with their strong ego and attachment, "My child should
be like this, like that."

—*Sachiko Weeden is a school proprietor*
from Japan.

❧

With all the changes which a little child brings along, I
lost the rhythm of life which I'd adopted during
pregnancy and didn't manage to meditate regularly any
more. I could feel how this affected me and made me
weaker. So I was very happy to be able to sit my second

ten-day course after one and a half years to recharge my
battery!

—*Susan Weber lives with her husband and baby*
daughter in Switzerland.

Amala, a well-known Indian actress, also took a retreat while pregnant with her first child:

Through pregnancy and delivery I practiced the
meditation, slowly discovering my inner strength,
working out my negativities and consciously radiating
mettā. I would have long communications of *mettā* with
the baby in my womb, welcoming it into the world and
offering it my love. All this may sound silly—but every
mother expecting a child has some profound experience
regarding the new life growing inside her. When Akhil
was born, he came with his eyes wide open and twinkling.
Everyone commented on how peaceful he was. I would
smile and say "He's a Dhamma baby."

During the course I strongly experienced the bond
between Akhil and myself. Dhamma helped me
understand that he does not belong to me. I am only his
caretaker—his guide. He is four and a half now. He has
always let me meditate morning and evening without
disturbance. At the most he comes quietly into the room
and lays his head on my lap till I finish or whispers what
he has to in my ear and I whisper back with my eyes closed.
Sometimes when he is terribly cranky, as four-year-olds
do get, I tell him he can quickly be happy if he watches
his breath. He closes his eyes for a few seconds and then
runs away happy. He may not consciously be doing what
I say, but at least he understands that it is a choice to be
unhappy or happy! He also understands the importance
of silence. My need to do more courses—going away for
ten days at a time —he accepts without any questions.
The separations have made him wiser and more
independent than most children his age. With anger and
impatience reducing through Vipassana and the power of

mettā, each day is a wonder and a joy for a mother and Dhamma baby.

Steve Rann is a builder and Gabrielle is an acupuncturist. They met in Australia, moved to rural Wales, then settled in England to bring up their family.

It's such an invaluable blessing having children . . . The mind is right there on the surface, but habitwise they're much like adults . . . .

It's fascinating to see how two boys with the same background can be so different, how their separate qualities are developed or quashed in different environments and that places a responsibility on us . . . .

Dhamma is something to share as a family, with friends and in our working lives. Knowing others who meditate, and who are just regular people having a fun time, is important for the children. When they're older and having to deal with things like alcohol and drugs, if they know people who don't use those things, it won't seem so weird . . . .

The children have helped me become more compassionate and patient with them, and with adults too . . . .

They've been such great teachers to us.

—*In conversation, the Rann family, Hereford UK*

Another Way To Grow

It is challenging at first but nevertheless enjoyable. It is good to look at oneself . . . .

Many people have different views about meditation. They think it is a waste of time. But if you do it sincerely you will always be goodnatured, honest and trustworthy and you will become a favorite with everyone . . . .

—*Postcourse feedback from young people.*

In India until recently meditation was associated with old age and retirement from active life. But now college students are the majority group attending Vipassana courses and a center has even been established on one college campus. Though meditation is not as yet a mainstream activity in the West, the program of young people's courses is expanding with very encouraging results. Schools are beset with increasing numbers of children with behavioral difficulties and attention deficit disorders. Anapana meditation has enormous potential for improving this situation, and as the benefits for youngsters of all ages become more widely known, interest will certainly spread.

Much that is offered to young people today is based on materialism and instant gratification of desires. Through meditation the young learn a different approach—a way of looking inside to resolve their problems. With the compass of meditation in their hands, they find a path that leads to their own happiness and the happiness of others.

Chapter 9

HEALING MIND—HEALTH AND VIPASSANA

Adventure: mountaineering, rock climbing, backpacking, white water rafting, canoeing, caving, abseiling, trucks, buses, cars, motorcycling, cycling, aeroplanes, helicopters, hitchhiking and travelling. I have tried all these for the experience, either in an attempt to conquer fear or to see how close I can get to the line, as I call it, or death: that great dread. In meditation death comes with every out breath, how much closer do you want to go?

—Nat Cohen took his first Vipassana course at Cyrenian House, a drug rehabilitation center in Perth, Australia where he was working as a charity collector.

Siddhartha Gotama grew up as a prince, surrounded by all the luxuries of the royal household. Though from childhood he preferred a meditative life, his father wanted him to become a great ruler. The king did his best to divert his son's attention to worldly things and to shield him from harsh everyday realities. However, the story goes that in successive outings the Buddha-to-be encountered a man withered with age, a sick man, a corpse and a monk. These incidents caused him to reflect on suffering and aspire to finding a way of liberation from it. He decided to abandon palace, family and career in a quest for truth. It was a six year journey, which took him beyond the extremes of indulgence and self torture to the practice of Vipassana and the attainment of full enlightenment as the Buddha.

149

Testing your limits with travel and adventure was once the preserve of eccentric individuals. Now, it seems, everyone's doing it. Sometimes explorers go full circle, like the Buddha, and find themselves. They come to understand that the outside world is pretty much all inside and that in meditation you meet the unexpurgated version of yourself and learn how to deal with it.

Body-Mind

What is this wellbeing that we seek? Good health requires a state of complete balance between body, mind and environment, dis-ease is what we get when that balance is lost. A combination of physical, mental and social factors makes up the whole person. Each one contributes to our evolving state of health. But of these mind is most important because it is the central directing force of our entire life and activity. Vipassana is a scientific technique of self observation, within the framework of one's own mind and body; a healing by observation of and participation in the universal laws of nature (Dhamma), that operates upon our thoughts, feelings, judgments and sensations. It aims at the total eradication of mental negativities and conditionings to achieve real peace of mind and to lead a happy, healthy life. Courses in Vipassana are open to people from any background with reasonably good physical and mental health. However even those who are sick can participate, provided the person is able to comply with the code of discipline, follow the meditation instructions and practice accordingly, and that the appropriate facilities and support are available at the center to cater for the individual's needs. Specially adapted Vipassana courses have successfully been given for visually impaired students, patients with leprosy, drug addicts and street children.

A wealth of evidence exists about the positive effects of Vipassana in a variety of health disorders, both physical and mental. Such health benefits are byproducts of deep meditation practice, not its main objective. Healing—not disease cure, but the essential healing of human suffering— is the purpose of Vipassana.

I was born with scoliosis, a spinal deformity. Most of my childhood years were spent in a body brace with three columns of stainless steel pushing out of my shirt collar, supporting a plaster chin rest and neck hold. I never got used to it and never came to terms with it. I developed my own mechanisms for survival and growth and managed to reach puberty with few apparent difficulties. However the onset of adolescence was a nightmare that was less easy to shrug off. At an early age I took to alcohol, drugs and generally kicked out at the old life of my childhood. By 14 I had been released from wearing the body brace but had entered another cage of my own creation, one of systematic body abuse. I started to travel and made the link with the Vipassana technique . . . .

For about nine years my life was settled. I worked, I had a relationship, I studied for my degree, and I became increasingly committed to the practice of Vipassana. The initial benefits that I had felt in the first couple of years of my practice, an increased sense of calm, a space separate from the usual world of reaction and turmoil, had moved on. In my practice, without making it in any way a focus, I was starting to unravel nearly thirty years of knots of tension that had built up around my deformity. It was a wonderful organic and natural releasing that was taking place. I started to notice that my own brand of misery was simply that, it was mine. Everyone else around me had their own difficulties, physical, mental, emotional, social, whatever it may be, no one was free of some difficulty. In fact it seemed that I was relatively free in comparison. As Goenkaji says, it is very easy to remain equanimous towards the grosser realities, it is the less obvious that are harder.

My long developed smiling-face attitude to my own deformity was now starting to have a real base of self-compassion and equanimity. My attitude to my own physical condition gradually became very clear. I was more bothered by the way I looked than the way I was. For all of my life I have been happy and comfortable to accept assistance wherever it is needed and offered, but I had never been able to accept that my body was deformed. This was a fundamental acceptance for me and was essential for me to actually make progress. Again, once I had faced this truth, it became easier to see how my daily practice and my increasing immersion into the Vipassana world was unraveling this most superficial but encaging of neuroses.

—Dave Lambert has served Vipassana courses in many different parts of the world.

Not long ago, things were very different for the healthy, confident young woman working for an export company, who loves life and studies and meditates in her free time.

Back in my teens eating disorders, bulimia then anorexia, developed. I made a suicide attempt and underwent psychiatric treatment in a number of hospitals. Alongside the medication for my symptoms, I began abusing other chemical substances and drugs as well as alcohol. By the age of 20 I was severely underweight and malnourished and suffered from extreme hormonal and biochemical imbalance. My menstrual cycle had ceased completely.

Despairing at ineffective treatments, mentally and physically exhausted, someone suggested I try Vipassana. Slow but substantial changes followed. It became clear to me that I needed to meditate more. After two years of practice and several courses, I became free of drugs of any kind and experienced great relief in my physical symptoms. Little by little, Dhamma is healing all aspects of my life.

—Laura Tolver, age 25, sat her first course in Nepal.

When I was still very young my father developed a brain tumour, went blind and subsequently died. Further to this, since early childhood I have had a stutter and of course suffered during my teens from a debilitating lack of self-confidence. Together these things left me with certain mental scars which continued to affect me in later years.

In my early twenties I went to university to study Philosophy and Anthropology and it was during this time that I first attended a course of Vipassana meditation. The technique that was taught offered a way of living in the moment with an attitude that developed a calming balance of mind which, I found, helped me develop self esteem and confidence. I realized that to a large degree my speech impediment was compounded by the anxiety and fear of finding myself in situations I would not be able to handle. As I continued the meditation practice, I found this fear and anxiety diminished slowly but steadily and the stutter lessened as a result.

Even though I had tried a number of speech therapies, I found their efficacy shallow and based on simple behavior modification without attending to root causes, while Vipassana dealt only with these root causes and left the changes in behavior to come naturally.

—*Tim Lewis, a builder and architectural designer, lives in Auckland, New Zealand with his longtime partner. They continue to practice Vipassana together.*

Unexpectedly at the age of 43, a meditator doctor had a stroke which left him without speech and the use of his legs. Lying in the ambulance, aware his life was at risk, he began to meditate. Within a few days he was mobile again and speech slowly started to return. Still, normal work was out of the question. In this predicament, who would pay the bills, see the children through college, support elderly parents? He attended a rehabilitation center for stroke victims but deep inside doubted he could overcome the disability. However, taking early retirement from his senior post, he continued to meditate with the support of family and friends. Within twelve months he underwent a remarkable recovery, sat a thirty-day retreat and was appointed an assistant teacher of Vipassana. Trauma somehow had produced a change for the better. He returned to work in opthalmics, his speciality, and money worries evaporated. Temperamentally, the old agitation and irritation was gone. There was a calm about him now and a special appreciation of every opportunity to meditate and to share his blessings in whatever way he could.

—Dr Sonny Oo lives with his family
in northern England.

Before my first course I suffered from frequent headaches, significantly high blood pressure and some menopausal symptoms. Since beginning to practice Vipassana meditation this has changed. I have not taken any analgesics, the headaches have decreased and my blood pressure is normal. The menopausal symptoms which I experienced as troublesome before (insomnia and mood changes) have eased or trouble me less. I find the daily practice of meditation very helpful in coping with the changes I am going through at present, enabling me to maintain or regain a sense of balance more easily than before and to act with more decisiveness.

Having worked as a nurse/midwife/counsellor in the health service for the last twenty years, I am aware of the need which exists for learning how to cope with stress. Vipassana offers a simple and clear way without unwanted side effects.

—Christa Wynn-Williams is a hospice nurse and
therapist in Scotland. For her meditation has
now become "a necessity, an attitude of
being still and not just in formal sitting."

An army dentist felt giddy one evening while playing badminton and fell down. He regained consciousness to discover he had developed a severe back and neck condition. Neither conventional painkillers nor complementary therapies brought lasting relief. As time passed by, physical deterioration brought on chronic depression and he became a shadow of his former self. He retired from military service, feeling jealous of those with successful careers and full of self pity. His physical condition worsened, the atmosphere at home grew increasingly tense and he seriously considered closing down his dental clinic. As a last resort, on the recommendation of a neighbor, he joined a ten-day Vipassana retreat, never thinking he'd be able to complete it. With faith and sheer willpower he learned to meditate and noticed an unmistakable lessening in the pain which had become his constant companion. It was the beginning of an amazing recovery. He returned home a new person— with a new mind in a new body. No more collars, traction, pegs, painkiller and sleeping pills. He took up brisk walking and gardening. After more than twelve years of agony, he rediscovered his profession and a renewed commitment to caring for his patients.

> —*Dr Lt Col M. Mohan Kumar lives and works in*
> *Andhra Pradesh, India.*

Vipassana has been repeatedly shown to help alleviate a range of psychosomatic disorders such as chronic pain, hypertension, bronchial asthma and peptic ulcers. Mind and body are constantly and inextricably related. It is as a by-product of the process of mental purification that many of these physical conditions are eased or eliminated. But we should take care not to make disease cure the goal of meditation.

In the case of mental health, Vipassana provides a general psychological pattern of positive states of mind rather than a response to any particular problem. From the Vipassana viewpoint, mental disorders result from the accumulation of large quantities of defilements in the mind. These show up as various types of craving and aversion. Anyone without a totally pure mind (and who can claim that?) has some mental problem or another. The difference between an individual with or without a mental disorder as defined in psychiatric terms is only a matter of degree. In the aversion spectrum such negativities include: anger, hatred, ill will, restlessness, anxiety, sadness, fear, guilt, inferiority and jealousy; while typical cravings include passion, ego, greed, arrogance, possessiveness and vanity.

Sitting silently in meditation, we learn to accept the deepest truths about ourselves. Working always within the framework of the body, images, thoughts and emotions naturally bubble up as we observe the breath and sensations. Simultaneously we are aware of our mental state and the direct physical reverberations at the body level. The mind may be in flood at times but, resisting the details and remaining calm and detached, we watch each wave rise and subside. With practice the entire stockpile of mental impurities is gradually reduced and our potential for fulfillment grows as old conditionings peel away. Working with Vipassana (along with family support and professional help as needed), we can heal ourselves and transform the quality of our lives.

When one considers my family history, with its many examples of melancholy and eccentric characters, including many a sleepwalker, it should have come as no surprise that during my adolescence I too was afflicted with what Winston Churchill described as "the black dog." Depression. And not the "I don't feel good today" condition, but rather the feeling that you have to carry your face around in a wheelbarrow to stop your jaw from dragging along the ground. One is lamed. People tell you to snap out of it because you are physically in good shape. You don't want to snap out, you want to snap back in.

It is a depressive phase that led me to the path. I became very ill a year after migrating from Australia to Germany. The thrill of living in a new environment had worn off and I was homesick and totally disorientated. Thankfully, I had made some very persistent new friends who kept on contacting me even though I was not well enough to go out and socialize. One of these new friends silently left some information about Vipassana on the cupboard in the hallway. I picked it up, read it and put it down again. What, 4:00 a.m.? What, no talking? What about the chemist's shop that I was swallowing every day in order to get me in and out of bed? Going to the supermarket to buy groceries was a major feat for me so how could I handle ten days of my own somewhat confusing inner dialogue?

To my surprise, I coped very well. But naturally completing the course did not put an end to my Western skepticism. I kept looking for a catch—but gave up after a while because there isn't one. It is so simple, pure and logical. Observe, remain equanimous. Everything passes, even depression. So why fret. And if you are fretting, observe the fretting.

"Vipassana Take Away"—integrating this wisdom and practice day to day—is not so simple. I really have to work at this and look to others for support and encouragement. But I'm no longer afraid when the black dog barks, then slinks into the distance.

—*Linda Muller took her course at Dhamma Geha,*
the German meditation center near Karlsruhe.

A survey of New Zealand Vipassana students was undertaken in 1994. Students who had attended one or more ten-day courses were asked to answer a questionnaire. The completed questionnaires were analyzed to examine the impact of the meditation practice over time on many aspects of people's lives. All categories of personal wellbeing, including physical health, stress reduction, sense of integrity, motivation, relationships and overall happiness, showed significant improvements. Students' ability to cope with adversity had markedly increased. Large decreases in the use of alcohol and drugs were recorded.

—Independent report by David Hodgson, statistical consultant, commissioned by the Vipassana Foundation Charitable Trust, New Zealand

I can't remember how young I was when I first started wishing I was dead. Most people have wished that at some point in their lives, but in my family suicide is almost a tradition. Many of my relatives have died that way, and almost everyone in my immediate family has attempted suicide. Mental imbalance also runs in my family, which is no wonder with self-destruction abounding as it does. So to me it was natural not only to be depressed all the time, but to consider suicide as a viable way out.

In my mid-twenties I finally actually attempted to end my life. I remember how unnatural it seemed, how biologically unsound. I was supposed to be doing my utmost to survive, and here I was, trying to slice away at the wrists of my very own body in order to murder it. It was a very bizarre experience, and I'm awfully glad it hurt so much that I passed out and didn't succeed.

Nevertheless, in spite of the clear image I had that night of how intrinsically wrong it was to put an end to myself, I still had no positive solution. If anything, it just seemed disappointing that it was so difficult to die, so I still held suicide as an option for when things got really bad again.

Then I discovered Vipassana meditation. An aunt of mine was a practitioner and kept me aware of the sittings without in the least pushing me to go. Finally, one summer I got the urge to try it out. I drove up to Mendocino (California)) on my own and embarked upon this exploration of truth which would cause me to never again turn to death as a solution to life's problems. Vipassana did indeed turn out to be my saviour. I worked very hard those ten days, and what I gained turned my head around completely. I found out the truth about life, about my life, and most of all, about real happiness— not fleeting, situational happiness, but *real* happiness; the happiness that is our inheritance as living beings. I learned about it, and I experienced it first hand. I had often read about meditation and all the wonderful effects it can have, and I believed in it implicitly. But only through sitting for ten whole days myself was I able to know these things first hand, and only through knowing them first hand was I able to change my life around.

I still suffer from depression sometimes. I think it's a genetic thing that I just have to live with. But I no longer look to death as my escape. And I don't search out pharmaceutical solutions, as most psychiatrists would have me do. In fact, I never go to psychiatrists or therapists anymore. I practice Vipassana meditation instead. And—true confession—I'm not always the most regular or disciplined practitioner. But I know it's there, and I remember what it taught me about the joy that abides in every atom of my being and the beings of everyone and everything else, and it makes me feel a sense of calm and unity that is not just a New Age "positive affirmations" pep talk, but rather the real thing. I *know* the truth now, viscerally, and nothing will ever get in the way of that knowledge.

I've never even considered suicide since I first experienced Vipassana meditation sixteen years ago—not even once. And with my track record, that's a miracle in itself.

—Susan Craig Winsberg is a musician,
a recording artist and composer in the USA.

Jagdish Kela, a 20 year-old postgraduate student in Mumbai, had been carrying a problem since being in high school four years earlier. His mind was obsessed with all kinds of thoughts and fantasies, mostly about dirt, sex and death. He had become compulsive about washing and touching and was hardly able to go to classes. At times he felt the urge to hurt people or break things, agitation overwhelmed him and he would cry. Antidepressant and other drugs prescribed by psychiatrists were only marginally effective.

After some prior preparation he was able to take a Vipassana retreat. A further two courses followed. Within fourteen months he was admitted to an engineering college, free of medication, and feeling very much better. In his own words:

> Earlier I tackled my inner thoughts wrongly by thinking about them or trying to solve them. Both would increase my anxiety. Suppressing my impulses only led to more restlessness. I kept tying new knots every moment in the process. The fundamental change with Vipassana is that now I have learned how to leave these thoughts alone, whatever their content may be. And working with my sensations, I realize that all those disturbing thoughts come from the depths to the surface of my mind to go out, provided I watch them without reacting. Now I realize how I had become a slave of my own mind.

During the last fifteen years my external living conditions more than once presented good occasions for sinking down in despair—or for deep mental growth in the face of existential problems. The death of my father thirteen years ago became a deep Dhamma experience for me. I was not—as I had always been fearing in regard to a situation like this—paralyzed by indescribable sorrow and sadness, but instead felt nothing but love and gratefulness.

I got a glimpse into what our senses are unable to grasp and learned to develop faith in the course of events, whatever direction life might lead me. After this I had several miscarriages; they taught me to let go of deep lying desires. Then about six years ago my mother's physical weakness and fast mental decline made it necessary to make arrangements for regular nursing and care for her— a nightmare for most people. The common task of caring for my mother, however, led to deep understanding and love between my sisters and myself, which had never been there before. Finally, five years ago, doctors diagnosed a cancerous disease in me, which cannot be cured. Since then I am more than ever aware that my lifetime is very valuable, and I often feel deep gratitude being able to enjoy living in the present moment with body and mind still intact—this present moment, to which I can always return with the help of Vipassana.

—*Brunhilde Becker lives with her*
meditator partner in Germany.

Tackling Addiction

Of all the problems currently confronting humankind, drug addiction or chemical dependency is one of the most widespread and serious. Respecting no barriers of country or class, it undermines individual health, warps relationships, torments families, stunts the economy, fosters crime and destroys peace in the community. Substance abuse is a complex disorder which in the case of addicts means an over-dependence that has become habitual, obsessive and compulsive, governing every aspect of the individual's life— physical, emotional, social and mental. Joe, an ex-addict from Australia, illustrates from his own experience:

Addiction, basically means escapism, escape from reality . . . you use insanity—the human insanity— escapism. With a drug addict someone's used the vehicle of drugs to escape. And it is a very, very powerful vehicle—much more powerful than just the unaided fantasy, for the average human being, getting into dreams, workaholism or TV. The drug motivation, the drug use, is much more powerful than anything else. When I use it because it's so powerful, it takes the escapism to a life-threatening degree. Whereas other motivators (like living for money, power, prestige) don't threaten your life.

What causes this driven behavior despite the direst consequences? Someone may start using drugs for a number of reasons but eventually drug use becomes a reaction to uncomfortable body sensations which result from the constant interconnection between mind and body, and the thoughts which accompany these interactions. One chases pleasant feelings to displace the unpleasant. A person doesn't get addicted to anything out there, or to some inherent quality of the drug itself; it just seems that way. People get addicted to their own sensations of the body. By taking a drug, a certain kind of biochemical process starts in the body and one feels a type of sensation, which one starts liking. One develops a craving for it, then a habit, and finally gets addicted to the sensation. Addiction feeds on itself: one wants to enjoy that sensation again and again. This is what happens in all types of addiction, not only with drugs and alcohol. The addiction is actually to one's own body sensations.

Vipassana can remove the roots of addiction—craving and aversion—which other methods of treatment scarcely touch. The technique works directly with sensations which are continuously in contact with the deepest level of the mind. Through meditation practice, drug addicts can learn to face suppressed feelings, along with unpleasant sensations, that start to rise out of their unconscious. Gradually the mind becomes more balanced, gaining strength and understanding. Little by little, they see reality as it is and past habit patterns are broken. However progress requires a strong will on the part of the individual both to come out of addiction and to work towards this goal by observing themselves at the level of sensations. Professional support also plays an important role in their recovery.

"Start Again," an Addiction Therapy Center in Zurich, Switzerland uses meditation as a key element in drug rehabilitation. The city is well known for its heavy drug scene but "Start Again" is a completely new kind of addiction clinic. Modern therapy methods from the West, including one to one counselling, systemic couple/family therapy and self help with Narcotics Anonymous, are combined with ancient techniques of mental development from the East. It is one of the few rehabilitation centers for addicts that does not use drug therapy. Daily practice of Anapana meditation to calm and concentrate the mind is essential. Once their situation has stabilized, clients may request to take a ten-day Vipassana retreat to deepen the healing process. In each such case, careful attention is given to preparing the individual for the course and to their aftercare. Around 60% of those who stay the full length of the twelve month program successfully reintegrate themselves socially and at work and have not used hard drugs for more than a year since leaving "Start Again." In the war with addiction, this is the front line.

One client on the program describes in a poem how mindfulness of breathing brings a rare sense of wholeness and a vision of recovery:

It feels
really nice
to simply breathe,
to feel, to be
and nature cleans my rooms almost on its own.
If I could only stick to it, turn back
and do what I really want.

🐾

Gaining the motivation to heal themselves is important for progress. Another client was able to work as the
clinic's night watchman, a responsibility which helped him
through hard times:

The first time I learned about Anapana was four and a
half years ago. It was not at all a technique of meditation
and spirituality as I expected it to be. I was hoping that I
would feel light and free. But my hopes, as well as my
urge to seek refuge in a world of illusion as I did when I
took drugs, were dashed. The Anapana technique turned
out to be hard work. As part of the rehabilitation program
"Start Again," I practiced Anapana twice a day.

After three months, I had an eight month long relapse,
after which I decided to take part in "Start Again" once
more. At that point I began to see more clearly that my
existence did not only consist of pleasant experiences.
Intellectually, I began to understand that I can find an
inner distance to my emotions through meditation and
that I do not have to react blindly to cravings and
aversions. I learned to understand that I am the person
responsible for my own life; I also began to see just how
much I acted out of self interest. After four months of
Anapana, I did my first ten-day Vipassana course and a
second one after another half a year.

Meditation, then, to me means to get in contact with
myself and my feelings without getting tangled up in
them, to experience my changes, to be more honest with
myself and therefore with other people as well. I try to
live up to the standards of Vipassana in my daily life. Again
and again, I try to take a step back from my feelings and
the realties which I've constructed in my mind. Sometimes
I manage quite well and as a result don't have to react in
such a blind and self-destructive manner anymore, because
I can observe and feel calm in the situation. What I realize
more and more is that I need to confront the world around
me and that I can no longer just sit there and wait.
Vipassana is not a world of illusion in which I can seek

refuge. It helps me have a good look at my life. By continuing regular meditation, I find it more and more difficult to escape reality and flee to a world of illusions.

🐌

Not that meditation alone can reform an addict. Skilled professional help with rehabilitation, the love of friends and family, a dogged personality—all play their part. Nik, a "Start Again" graduate, explains:

Without a doubt, Vipassana meditation has contributed to my total abstinence from drugs, which I have been able to maintain for five years.

My understanding of Vipassana is to use it as a practical tool and a technique, I do not associate it with belief or religion. By observing my body and my feelings, I experience the relativity, the uniqueness, the transitoriness and the different dimensions of my self, fresher and clearer each time. It seems that one of the specific results of meditation is overcoming the feeling of desire and allowing the spirit to make decisions free from constraint.

Letting Go

Of all the changes awaiting us, death is the greatest. Since birth, this bookend has infused our existence with meaning, but mostly we avoid looking directly at that situation when "I" cease to be. When the body gives way and the mind goes out. When every possession is left behind and every desire is swept aside. Perhaps tomorrow, or in thirty years, we will die. Are we ready? Whenever it comes, can we rise to the occasion, meeting our end consciously and harmoniously, with all the wisdom of a lifetime? Nothing is more natural than dying, we know, just part of an ageless cycle. Yet how easy to lose perspective when someone dear passes away or we miss something precious. Grief reminds us of our own mortality: "I am also not forever."

Practicing Vipassana we engage in an ongoing process of learning. Body and mind rise and pass with each breath and every sensation. Repeatedly probing this truth within ourselves, we begin to accept it. Impermanence as felt experience dissolves the tendency to cling to what is "ours." Kindness and giving displace self-centeredness. Living a full and wholesome life, we prepare to make a good death.

An experienced meditator, Harsh Jyoti, found out in July 1992 that he had lung cancer and died in January 1993. Every time he had a setback (which happened quite often), from the first diagnosis and during his treatment, Vipassana helped him to restore his balance of mind. His son was able to observe him closely during the final period of his life.

I think Dhamma was protecting him. I think that was a very profound effect that we could see, even in the last stages. Whenever we said, "Do you want to meditate?" he would just nod his head, so all of us would sit around him and try to send *mettā* for twenty or thirty minutes. At one time he was fighting the disease, hopeful as we all were, that he would get a couple more years, then a couple more months, couple more weeks. But at some point during that last hospital visit, it probably just dawned on him that now he didn't have too much time, and he just accepted that and along with it the attachment to this life. And I think, probably because of that, his death was so smooth and so peaceful, because there was no fighting, no struggle, nothing.

My father suffered from high blood pressure. It started out about 150/90, then 120/80, then down to 110/70 and then 90/60 and all the while you could see his face—we have some photographs—very peaceful, sleeping happily. My brother had come back for our father's last few hours and we were watching him, just breathing, breathing and all of a sudden, it looked as though there was a small flicker, and that was it. It felt so peaceful. And although that was an occasion of great sorrow for us, seeing how peacefully he passed away, that gave us so much strength and consolation. Even my mother who was so close to him and normally a very emotional person, even she was in control of herself at that moment. It was like putting water in a saucer and letting it evaporate; he passed away without a ripple.

This, I feel, is how Dhamma protects. Dhamma doesn't protect us by not making us fall sick. All of us have to fall sick. It doesn't protect us by not making us die, because all of us have to die. But, whenever that happens, when you fall sick or die, you do it so peacefully and calmly.

I was almost 70 when I took my first Vipassana course together with Poul, my husband, who had Parkinson's disease. When we arrived home everyone could see the change. My husband looked much better and his speech had improved. For me the course marked a turning point. Having searched for so long, I knew that finally I had found my way of living.

The following year the two of us went on holiday to Gambia, where we enjoyed the sun and sea. Then one day while playing in the shallows, we were suddenly parted by a huge wave and an unusually strong underwater current which caught Poul and dragged him away. Even with the greatest effort, it took too long to reach him—it felt like an eternity before I finally succeeded and got him in to where I could stand. Too late—he had drowned. Finally people saw us and came to help. A young German gave Poul first aid, but with such force that he broke two ribs and his spleen was punctured. An ambulance arrived and we were taken to a hospital where they extracted the liquid from his lungs. They told me there was no chance he would survive. We were then moved to a private hospital and he was immediately placed in intensive care. What a night—with those gloomy prospects. When I asked Poul if he knew what had happened, he answered: "I drowned. It was wonderful to be dead, I hovered, gliding so happily, but as I could see you struggling with me below, I wanted to come down and help you."

Whatever might happen later, this was a loving way to take leave rather than death by drowning. Together we meditated and were lucky, the bleeding stopped by itself. However it took five long weeks before we were flown back to Denmark and he was admitted to hospital for checkups and rehabilitation. The doctors recommended he go to a specialized nursing facility, but my daughter and I decided to keep and nurse him at home.

Six months after the accident I travelled to the USA, first to visit family and then to take another much-needed Vipassana retreat. My concentration during the course was so strong that I got a very strange feeling of being dissolved in millions of small bubbles, that raced around and through me. This experience helped me immensely two years later, when I was able to tell both my husband and my two only brothers, how important it was to be at ease and peaceful at the moment of death. The three of them passed away in the same week—just before Christmas 1995. Despite this, because of my meditation, I remained calm and balanced. I was able to support the family and help us all to begin an active new life.

—Muguet Huffeldt lives in Denmark and was one
of the organizers of the first Vipassana
courses in that country.

❧

Anne first met Graham Gambie while travelling in India in the late 1970s. Meditation wasn't at all on her agenda then and he encouraged her to sit a Vipassana course. Sensing she was onto something good, Anne continued to meditate and serve at *Dhamma Giri* before heading off to Japan for work. Two years later she returned to the Igatpuri center and met Graham again when they served on the same course together. Within a couple of months, much to her astonishment, they were married.

She and Graham returned to Australia where he worked as an investigative journalist and took unpaid leave to conduct Vipassana courses as a newly appointed assistant teacher. Meditating and working together, the storms of the early days gave way to a deep sense of caring and togetherness. Like a new pair of shoes continually worn, the relationship in time became very comfortable.

On one particular ten-day course we were conducting together, I noticed that Graham, my husband at that time, was uncharacteristically missing words and slurring his speech. I became very concerned for his health and we made an appointment to see a neurologist the day the course ended. CT scans were taken of the brain and while waiting for the results we went for an enjoyable lunch. "Oh, it's nothing—nothing to worry about," I remember saying as we handed the folder to the neurologist. Without a word he removed the scans and placed them on the display panel. The photos showed a brain tumor which seemed at least 50% of the left hemisphere and on top of the tumor was a very large cyst.

I was numb and uncomprehending. Yes, we would cancel our air tickets to New Zealand. Yes, we could get Graham directly into hospital that afternoon. The numbness turned to tears as I phoned to arrange accommodation in Sydney with dear friends. Graham had to take the telephone receiver as I wasn't making any sense and make the arrangements himself. He was calm and collected.

While getting Graham into hospital and making sure he was comfortable I somehow managed outwardly to be cheerful. But as soon as I left his company I was back in tears again. That night as I meditated a deep sense of peace arose and it was to stay with me throughout Graham's ordeal. It was not the peace that comes through rationalization or intellectualization. It was just something that "kicked in." Within two days Graham was under the operating knife. They were not able to remove all the tumour. The prognosis was not good. The neurosurgeon told Graham that due to the nature of the tumour, an astrocytoma, he had maximum five years to live and, by the end of it, mentally he would be a vegetable.

Such news was devastating yet he took it in his stride. I once heard him say to visitors, "How can I be attached to this body and this mind when it is so constantly changing. There is nothing to hold on to." Workmates, friends, those who he knew through meditation would come and visit him. As one colleague said, "I came expecting to see a body on the bed and to console him. Instead I ended up telling him all about my problems and forgot about his." The days passed and I am grateful to have spent every one of them with him. He was discharged from hospital but within a week or so was back in again. He was having difficulty with his legs. They had become so tender and he could not walk far . . . .

It was June 27th, six weeks since the tumor was diagnosed, and I think both of us knew that this was to be the day he'd die. There would be no popping out of the hospital to run errands. We had a lovely day together and that night as I said goodbye I felt I couldn't get close enough to him. I hopped up on the side of the bed and began to put lipstick on. He asked why and I said it was because I wanted to look good for him. He then proceeded to say the nicest things about what a wonderful wife I had been and how he felt. I was happy and he was happy. We said goodbye. That night after dinner I was enjoying the last sip of hot chocolate. I took a breath and at that moment experienced such a deep sense of absolute peace and tranquillity. The phone rang. It was a junior nurse calling. Could I come in quickly, Graham was having a heart attack. It was clear that there was no need to hurry. Graham was gone.

I travelled to the hospital. It was late on Friday night. The neon lights shone and people were out strolling, window shopping, eating. A strong sense of fear and vulnerability arose within. Such a casual picture of life was not to be trusted. What seemed so real, so permanent, was nothing more than an illusion. We were all walking on very thin ice, blind to the knowledge that we could fall through at any given moment. The journey continued. We arrived at the hospital.

We proceeded upstairs to where the two of us had exchanged words only hours before. On entering the room alone I was immediately struck by the vibrancy of the atmosphere. Graham's body lay on the bed. It was very clear there was no one there. It looked like a cast off coat that could no longer serve its owner. This was all that remained of the person with whom I had just spent four very special years of my life.

What a wonderful life he had lived. I received letters from people who knew him in the past. Each one recounted something that Graham had done to help them in their life. I heard from others about when he was travelling in India, how he would give his last rupee to someone who needed it, how he used to feed the street children with money he received from a small investment he had. And then when I saw how much he had loved and helped others in the time we had together, it became very clear that all the wonderful good deeds he had done in his life, they had all gone with him.

There were no tears. How could there be tears? The relationship had gone full circle. There was nothing left unresolved or unsaid. Yes, it has been the hardest thing I have done in my life, but the fruits were so great and so numerous. I was truly fortunate to have shared my life briefly with such a human being.

The funeral was held. The pews were full and people lined the walls. They came from all persuasions, from all walks of life, each with his or her own personal reason for being there. It was strange to return home, to see his clothes just as he had left them and to know that there was no one there to claim ownership.

It is now twenty years since I sat my first course in Vipassana. So much has changed and so many

experiences—some very pleasant, some very painful—
have come and gone. Yet the practice of Vipassana has
endured. Not only has it endured, it has provided great
sustenance and shelter and above all a sense of
contentment and clarity not bound by the vicissitudes of
life.

> —*Anne Doneman remarried in 1991 and is a*
> *working mother with two children.*

Everything is changing
In a constant ripple
Of waves, of wind passing by.
Now is the time to be free from my "self"
not hoarding what I have, but tasting, letting go
not pushing away, but letting go on the sweet wind.

> —*Nature regularly features in Sachiko Aoi's poems.*
> *She sat her first retreat at Dhamma Bhānu,*
> *Japan in 1998.*

Chapter 10

MANAGING ONESELF—
VIPASSANA, WORK & SOCIAL ACTION

Most of us want to make a difference—in relationships, at work, to the wellbeing of the planet. We have energy, skills and experiences to contribute and there is special satisfaction when our efforts bring about good. Often we'd like to do more but somehow our actions don't match those fine intentions we have. Political, social and economic problems have always existed but with today's almost instant communications, we can see just how widespread these are: the frightened refugees vowing revenge, another tainted food scare, the latest corruption scandal. Why even now, we may ask, do these same patterns keep recurring? Why have world organizations like the U.N. and individual governments not been able to deal effectively with problems such as communal tension, poverty, unemployment and abuse of power? Do we ever learn?

One answer is that we are dealing with symptoms, the outward manifestations of these problems, not with the underlying causes—the greed, hatred and other negative feelings that pervade the world. Problems may seem to disappear but because the underlying sickness persists, the symptoms keep appearing again and again.

Then the people whose task it is to implement solutions through social structures or legislation may not have the necessary love and compassion to achieve their goal. Government organizations, for instance, often deal with problems in a distant and superficial manner and intended results are not achieved.

Vipassana offers an alternative approach to solving these problems and the untold misery they cause. Know-how and resources are certainly necessary but above all wisdom is required. By applying the benefits of meditation in a practical way, the problems can be tackled at two levels. Ultimately the solution has to be found at the individual level, each of us working on ourselves in a sustained campaign to remove negativity from our own minds, so that our personal input in different situations is as constructive as possible. Simultaneously we can also operate at the institutional level, encouraging the development of Dhamma principles and practices in corporate, professional, bureaucratic and political organizations. By their own example, meditators sometimes inspire others to change themselves; they can also initiate or add momentum to positive changes, small or large, across the spectrum of society.

❦

My friends say that I have changed for the better. Have I? Though the answer is quite simply "yes," the process of change was very difficult. Though my understanding of the inner self and awareness of the outer world was quite limited, I used to dream of doing something good for society. Why and how I never knew. I vividly remember in class seven when I read about the Green Revolution, which brought radical changes to agricultural output in northern India, I started dreaming of replicating that success in my home state, Bihar. By the time I was 13 years old I got fascinated by Communist Party ideology and in the 1989 general elections I worked to mobilize support for this Party.

I wanted to do something big. Of course I wanted to do so many things, but what did I do? I could not do anything and the worst was that my academic performance deteriorated. Despite the potential and also the desire to do well, my final result was so dismal. Due to various negativities I couldn't do anything in the proper way.

I am still unable to believe that a simple meditation technique like Vipassana can do such a wonder for me. It has given me a solution to each and every problem. I don't claim that now I am free from all negativity but certainly today I know how to deal with it. My concentration has gone up and with it my understanding of events is deeper. Due to proper understanding now I respond to any event in a better way. Vipassana has taught me how to stay cool and do my job effectively. Every day I try to improve upon the last. I am sure that if I keep on practicing Vipassana I will certainly realize my dream of doing something good.

—*Durgesh Kedia is an M.B.A. student*
in Pune, India.

I have never wanted to just "do a job." For as long as I can remember I have needed to feel that whatever I am doing is making a difference, is something (even if only a tiny something) that will leave the world a better place after me. And I love my work as an environmental scientist (soil erosion, actually). It brings twin delights: knowing that my daily labors contribute a little to the long slow business of making the planet healthy again, and discovering the wonders hidden in even the most taken-for-granted of natural processes. How many times have I marvelled at the way muddy water flows into puddles!

Anyway, that's how I feel on good days. On bad days, no matter how much I remind myself of the big picture, the crushing weight of academic bureaucracy and institutionalized power-gaming overwhelms me. Futility rules: why am I doing all this? It is then that my Vipassana helps me most. It helps me to be "there," to concentrate on what I am actually doing (rather than what I imagine I am contributing to or imagine I am battling against).

What is that phrase? "Contentless hope." It fills my meditation and spills out into the rest of my life, like water spills out of the puddle. And I go along with it and am less hopeless.

*—Dr David Favis-Mortlock is a researcher at the
Environmental Change Institute,
University of Oxford, UK.*

Work To Do

Strength of personality is an important prerequisite for responsible social action. The foundation for a person's character and their progress, both worldly and spiritual, lies in one's moral qualities. Observing the five precepts—doing one's best not to kill, steal, lie, commit sexual misconduct or take intoxicants—is a part of the technique of meditation. But this baseline of morality extends beyond the Vipassana course itself. Maintaining and developing our own moral sensibility is particularly important in helping us successfully overcome the pressures and difficulties of everyday life. We attempt to avoid harming others with hurtful physical actions or words. We try instead to be kind and understanding in our dealings, to respect all life, to be generous, open and truthful. Right livelihood, making a living in line with the moral precepts, is also part of the path. Everyone needs money, but how to earn it without harming oneself or others in the process? Sitting daily with Vipassana and applying it in the workplace, we begin to see what is possible.

Building is now just all business really. I'm more or less a businessman, I guess. I can still hold a hammer, hit the nail on the head, but I think being careful about dealings with money and people is most important because it's their big commitment in life to build a house or whatever and it's your responsibility to make sure it goes right.

There's a lot of difficulty doing the right thing in the world where everybody's out to get what they can. So you feel like, "I'll have to grab so that I'm just equal to the others. I'm not really ripping anybody off, I'm just grabbing my share of the cake, because it's going so quickly before my eyes that soon I'll be only left with the crumbs. All the responsibility and only crumbs."

But it's not really like that. It's fair. It has to be fair. And in fair dealing you have to take control. You're the builder or you're the business person. You're the one that sets the deal and you have to set it right for yourself and stick by it. That way you set it right with everyone else as well. It's taken me a long time. It's very difficult. But by practicing Vipassana, being grounded in moral principles it gets ingrained so that you start living properly; instead of thinking you live properly or talking about living properly, you *live* properly. And then your relationships with other people benefit and you're more at peace with yourself.

—*In conversation, Jim Talbot from southern Australia*

A world-class sportsman, Bishen Singh Bedi represented India in the national cricket squad for many years.

Cricket is a way of life and I see so much similarity with Vipassana. Both involve applying a fairly consistent amount of concentration and effort over a period of time. When we say that someone is not playing cricket, it means that he is not being fair in life, he is not upright, he is not honest. As the late Prime Minister of Australia, Sir Robert Menzies, once said: "If only America and Russia played cricket, this world would be a much happier place to live in."

To me, what we are taught in a Vipassana course is a "psyching process," how to peak yourself up at the right moment. I had many limitations with my own cricketing ability and I can tell you—great players like Sunil Gavaskar and Kapil Dev—how they psyched themselves up, and then had pride in their performance. When I say "pride," that should not be taken in a sense of conceit or arrogance. This "pride" means satisfaction at your personal performance. If you're not proud of yourself, nobody else is going to be proud of you. And this personal pride should be followed by something called national pride.

Personally I have learned life is a never-ending process of learning and I have learned from Vipassana that I can introduce this technique to young kids whom I am training from 10 to 15 years of age: to improve concentration, to inculcate some kind of belief in their own ability and some kind of discipline which cricket requires for the betterment of their own personality and for the betterment of the society in which they are going to grow up. And also I may add, to eliminate the possibility of ball tampering, betting and bribery, I'm sure this technique would help to a great extent.

My daily work requires a high level of commitment and good organizational skills. I am the Director of a five years young organization which has grown very rapidly and has five major projects, four of which are businesses distinctly different in nature and set in different localities. They include a plant nursery and landscaping business, a café and lunch delivery service, a family relations center and a counselling and consulting center. The two "non-counselling type" businesses are in fact training "unemployable" young people in life and work skills so that they are employable and have a clear sense of purpose and direction.

I find that the regular practice of Vipassana allows me to deal effectively with tensions which arise in my day to day work, enables me to get unstressed quickly, helps me to stay more balanced and assists me to deal with issues with greater insight. Vipassana meditation is an excellent tool for self-therapy.

I have a greater understanding of cause and effect and most of the time I am able to examine my own motives and reactions without those reactions spilling uncontrollably onto others. I think I am more compassionate—towards myself as well as others—and I am also able to take firm action and speak openly and truthfully. I believe I promote the conduct of the organization's business in an ethical and principled manner.

—*Brenda Nancarrow lives in Queensland, Australia.*

Roop Jyoti, a Harvard Ph.D, is Vice Chairman of his family's business empire and an advisor on administrative reforms and economic policies to the government in Nepal.

Vipassana is relevant to all sections of our society and all types of human activities. It is certainly relevant to the business world, to the world of trade and commerce, to the world of manufacturing, to the world of economic activities.

Vipassana teaches how to tackle ups and downs in life calmly. One engages in trade and the price sometimes goes up and sometimes goes down. One engages in manufacturing and one is faced with problems and uncertainties all around—production problems, labor problems, raw material problems, marketing problems, finance problems and it goes on. One may engage in any type of business activity and there are always problems, there are always uncertainties, there are always ups and downs. We were expecting sales to go up but they go down. We were hoping the profits to rise but they decline. We are expecting the interest rates to go down but they go up. We are expecting the cost of goods sold to decrease but they increase. Are we able to deal with such situations calmly? Most certainly, if we are practicing Vipassana and applying it in our daily lives.

Vipassana teaches how not to get upset in life. Business management involves dealing with people, good people, bad people, all kinds of people. Some behave decently, some don't. Some are satisfied customers, some aren't. Some are reliable workers, some aren't. Amidst this maze of uncertainty, there is one certainty—we don't have a choice of people we get to deal with. Whether we like our superiors or not. Whether we like our subordinates or not. Whether we like our working conditions or not. Whether we like the task assigned to us or not. We may not have any immediate options. Does it help to get upset? No, it only makes things worse, not only for ourselves but also for those around us. But we do just that unless we have learned Vipassana meditation and are practicing it regularly.

Vipassana teaches how not to react in the face of provocation. Friendly meetings turn into shouting matches. Nice customers suddenly get angry. Employees don't do what they are told to do. Workers make impractical, unrealistic demands. Bosses give unreasonable, impossible tasks. Do we get provoked and react with a fit of temper? That's what we tend to do which makes the situation worse for ourselves and for others, unless we are trained in Vipassana meditation and have learned to observe our sensations, the natural vibrations within ourselves.

Vipassana provides us with a skill to deal with all types of situations in life with serenity, tranquillity, and equanimity. There could not be another sphere of life where such a skill is of more utility, of more relevance, of more importance, than the corporate world.

As a business man, the profit motive, the desire to make money, is still there. Profit for whom? is the key question. As I've grown in Dhamma, my attitude has gradually changed. It seems to me now that it's necessary to run and grow a successful business because it can help so many people, from one's own immediate family to thousands of families who are getting a livelihood from different enterprises and the banks and shareholders. For our own needs we could easily live off the income from property, but that would not be fulfilling our proper responsibilities, so we keep taking on new projects.

Above all, as someone who is successful, rich and famous, you have to beware inflating your ego. There are so many temptations, intentional or otherwise, for oneself and one's children also. The technique of Vipassana is particularly important in helping to manage oneself and keep the ego down to size.

Vipassana teaches us how to be responsible without developing attachment. Vipassana does not make us indifferent, it makes us more aware of our responsibilities. Vipassana trains us how not to react involuntarily but how to be properly proactive. Vipassana does not make us unambitious, it makes us more resourceful. Vipassana teaches us how to tolerate short-term pains for the long-term gains. Vipassana develops our will power to persist with the right actions, it makes us more patient, more persevering. Vipassana makes us capable of doing all this by making us become aware of our inner self. With Vipassana we get rid of our negativities and purify our mind and a pure mind guided by pure Dhamma always makes the right decision, always takes the right actions.

It's very high pressure, particularly for a professional woman trying to have an independent life outside of work. Before the course, I found it impossible to prioritize, couldn't judge for myself what was important, didn't really know who I was or how stressed out I got until I was actually near the falling point. In Vipassana I found a bridge. The connection between mind and body, intangible emotions with tangible sensations. The connection between who I am and who I want to be. It's just a beginning, a small step towards balance.

—*Nita Souhami lives in New York and works at a bank in Wall Street.*

India today is carving out a role as a world leader in software and other fields of engineering. In the city of Mumbai, Anand Engineers has adopted a novel approach.

During the early 1990s this chemical engineering company employing 100 staff and workers set up a research project on the effect of Vipassana on business management.

Jayantilal Shah, the managing director at Anand Engineers, had long been convinced of the link between inner development and material prosperity. Vipassana meditation, he felt on the basis of his own experience, offered a method to achieve this ambitious goal. As he repeatedly attended retreats each year, the changes in his behavior and attitude were appreciated by fellow directors who also started meditating. Paid leave was offered to anyone wanting to learn the technique and more than 75% of company personnel have now taken a ten-day course.

As minds slowly shifted and old habits with them, material results began to follow. The positive changes in individuals through meditation helped to improve the quality of interpersonal relations at every level in the company. Dispassionately reviewing their own role, the directors realized that arrogance in their attitude to the workforce led to insecurity and a lack of trust on both sides. Little by little, contractual obligations became converted into real relationships. When fatigue stress, resulting from prolonged illness in the family, gave rise to erratic behavior in a senior member of staff, special care and sympathy were given to her. In another case, an unskilled worker was due to be sacked for shoddy work and being uncooperative. However closer investigation revealed that the company had been expecting the man to take on other duties without recognition. As a result he was offered a new post and all grievances vanished. Many decisions which were previously being imposed by the directors are now being transferred to self-managing teams. Teamwork and counselling help to reduce conflicts in the organization, motivation and a sense of shared responsibility have grown and the company as a whole has become more harmonious and productive.

Since the opportunity to learn Vipassana was offered to the workforce in the mid 1980s, there has been no industrial unrest or strike at the company. Supervisors show greater understanding and respect for workers and all report reduced stress due to better communication and greater job satisfaction. Overall improvements in the working environment have meant that the business has expanded, with turnover growing tenfold over a decade and increased profits to match. However the company's emphasis has also moved with the times, beyond pursuit of the bottom-line, to a broader, deeper vision of wealth creation—including money, health, joyful working relationships and peace of mind. Free welfare programs and a meditation space at the plant also play their part in creating a living, working community.

Unforeseen events during 1999 severely tested the company's mission and working practices. A boycott of Indian products by the U.S. Administration following nuclear testing on the subcontinent, combined with the Indian Government's own policy of globalization and liberalization, totally transformed Anand Engineers' trading environment. Business was slashed by 40% and healthy profits turned overnight into heavy losses. Everyone felt the pinch, but equanimity not panic prevailed. Deep cuts in salaries were introduced, with directors taking the lead. Layoffs across the company were amicably agreed, reducing the workforce by one quarter. Restructuring plans including investment in new technologies were rapidly brought forward. Despite the steep learning curve, they are confident that the new-look company will perform well in the global marketplace.

The experience of a number of business enterprises has shown that the introduction of Vipassana meditation to the people in the organization has improved the working atmosphere, the cooperative attitudes and the harmony within. Managers have become more patient in dealing with business uncertainties and more tolerant in dealing with employees' difficulties. Workers have become more reliable and capable of carrying out their tasks, even if they entailed repetitious and monotonous routines. Observing the benefits of Vipassana, many business and nonbusiness organizations have begun providing paid leave to their employees to attend Vipassana meditation courses. Some have treated Vipassana as a training program, some have included it in their Human Resource Development activity and yet others have simply considered it as an aspect of employee welfare. Vipassana has reduced instances of confrontation and situations where conflicts arise unnecessarily. Vipassana helps a person live happily and happy individuals make a happy organization. Employees become grateful towards their employers for giving them the opportunity to learn Vipassana and employers reap the rewards in the form of higher productivity and better morale.

As the manager of a small company I now promote an atmosphere that is more conducive to teamwork and individual decision-making. My management and negotiation style has changed from a more strict to a more supportive and flexible one. The response from the team and our customers has been positive. The employees take more responsibility and are better prepared to make their own decisions. We have become more successful since the customers awarded us with more business.

—*Joachim Rehbein from New Zealand took his first course in 1990 and has been meditating ever since.*

So, what's the word for someone who is behaving in a neurotic and paranoid fashion? Whatever it is, that was me after committing to meditate for ten days (ten hours a day!) in silence.

I wouldn't say that I'm a total novice at this new age stuff. I've done yoga, but a real workout is still a good run and a set of weights. I attend some spiritual service or meeting every week and have visited almost every denomination of service I can imagine. In fact, to the point, I once visited a Buddhist temple and sat for a half hour of meditation. I can sum up the experience in one word, claustrophobic. Ten days? After about ten minutes, I thought I couldn't breathe.

Yet, even with my one less than fulfilling meditation experience, here I was packing off to a Vipassana meditation retreat. It all started out when I decided to leave my job in March. Everyone told me, "Keith, take a few months off to clear your mind." So, in typical type-A form, I tried to find a way to cram three months of mind clearing time into the fewest days. Then I remembered a talk I heard at The World Economic Forum meeting in Davos. Camped out in the hills of Switzerland for a week with a couple of thousand of your closest world leader friends is Davos, and among the powwows on economics and politics was an oversubscribed panel session entitled "Happiness." I guess great power and money do not necessarily guarantee you happiness. So we were there to hear S. N. Goenka promise happiness if we followed this ancient tradition of meditation which can only be taught in a concentrated ten-day course. Being happily (at least frantically) employed at the time, I thought there was no way I'd get ten days away from work. So, now, with some time on my hands and the desire to find happiness and clarity in fewer than three months, I focused on giving Vipassana a try. The other thing that made this interesting was my belief that anything that terrified me this much had to yield some powerful results. Or, of course, it could always send me screaming into the woods after a half hour.

As one who has been in the middle of a career search, so much of my energy had been put into finding the next move that "made sense." Sense is defined as the next obvious step up the career ladder. As the youngest Chief

Marketing Officer in the Fortune 500, I couldn't take a job that wasn't higher up the corporate food chain in either position or company. If I did, I'd look like a loser, wouldn't I? It became clear to me that I had created a gallery of phantom spectators who I looked to for approval of my career moves. What would make me happy? What kind of question is that?

Day six was a nightmare. Each time the hour sitting would draw to a close, we would hear Goenka begin to chant which usually lasted a few minutes, but at least we knew it was over. However, there was one really long note that he would hold at the end of the chant. It was in Pāli, an ancient Indian language, the word was probably "love" or something. I swear, that note seemed to get longer and longer each time. By the last sitting at the end of the seventh day I was sure that the sadistic little Goenka was drawing that love word out on purpose to prolong the pain. Then, I'd open my eyes and see the guy there with a look of peace and realize, there go my aversions. And I guess that's the point of this entire exercise. We were practicing the same thing that we live every day. In meditation we were experiencing the very physical sensations that we would have in real life when someone insulted us or frustrated us. In meditation we were learning to watch those impermanent sensations and let them pass. Not dwelling on them and making them worse. Of course, we also learned what would happen when we did dwell on them. When I concentrated on the pain in my knee and got angry, it only multiplied the pain. Sounds like the compounded frustration I feel when I think about how angry my boss has made me. However, when I would "calmly, quietly, patiently, persistently, conscientiously, repeatedly just observe," the pain would pass. There was a real lesson here for my daily life.

Hours and hours of good and bad memories and fantasies were experienced. There were also distracted times during meditation that I was at my creative peak.

So, where do I go from here since I've been home? I'm giving a maintenance level of meditation a try. I'm not sure if I'm going to give up my Bordeaux collection just yet or stop participating in the industry of killing animals for food, but I would say that I got enough not to turn my back on the opportunity for greater happiness. So, I'll keep being aware, observing and not reacting.

—*Keith Ferazzi is now the president and CEO of YaYa, an internet advertising company.*

Helping Hands

People engaged in various fields of social work or the helping professions have the chance to make a direct impact on the daily lives of others. Doctors, nurses, teachers, psychologists, counsellors and others, all seek to use their talents for our benefit. Noble occupations maybe, but they carry their own risks. Not just on account of pressing need and external working conditions but because constant interaction with suffering in others can trigger one's own weaknesses, sucking the helper into the same whirlpool of misery as the client. Vipassana meditation offers a mechanism for functioning sympathetically and effectively in demanding social situations, while protecting oneself and replenishing one's own mental resources.

It was not long after I had started practicing Vipassana that I had the opportunity to put it into practice in a challenging environment, as a periodic detention supervisor for the New Zealand Justice Department. Periodic detention is a corrective measure which requires the detainees to give up part of their valued weekend to do compulsory community service. It is a punishment one step removed from imprisonment as a result of having committed crimes such as assault, theft and disorderly behavior.

I'm not sure why I was selected for the job instead of my burly bearded Greek friend who looked like someone not to be messed around with. I, on the other hand, gave the opposite impression of being timid, unassertive and rather green to the ways of the world. That was my impression at least.

On my first day at work, not knowing what to expect, I arrived at the detention center nervously early. It was a foot-stamping frigid morning as the warden rattled out a snappy roll call. It fractured the chilly air but not the icy glare of the detainees. The varying degrees of resentment and sullen aversion suggested that they did not take kindly to their new supervisor. What did they have in store for me?

I was in charge of a dozen detainees. Our task for the day was to clear scrubby bush at a school. With some cause for concern I took an inventory of the pitchforks, slashers, picks, axes, spades and other sharp implements as they were being loaded into the van. The warden must have had a lot of trust in the thick skin of his supervisors. It was not hard to imagine being perfunctorily dispatched in a shallow roadside grave on the way. Fortunately all these fears did not materialize. I found I could do the job quite well, being equipped with a certain amount of equanimity and quiet compassion which the practice of Vipassana develops. There were no untoward incidents to speak of during my period of employment.

However, because of the tense working environment it was inevitable that stress accumulated during the day. I came to realize very clearly the great value of the daily morning and evening practice of Vipassana. When I returned home and started meditating there was often an immediate explosive release of the day's stress. It was almost unbelievable. It certainly convinced me that Vipassana is a wonderful mental bath at all levels and an ideal tool for people engaged in demanding fields of social work.

—*Richard Rossi has been sitting in this tradition for twenty-five years.*

Thomas Crisman had been practicing law in the United States for about ten years when he took his first Vipassana meditation course in 1980. After graduation from engineering school in 1965 and from law school in 1969 he began practicing intellectual property law, a field specializing in patent, trademark and copyright law, in Dallas, Texas. Most of his law practice up until his first course had been involved with litigation; that is, the representation of clients in lawsuits with other parties over amounts of money that were significant and over issues about which both parties frequently became very emotionally involved.

Litigation in the United States during the last few decades has been characterized by the aggressiveness with which the lawyers represent their clients and the so-called "hard ball" tactics that they employ in order to frustrate and obtain an advantage over the lawyers representing the opposing side. In my own legal career I wholeheartedly embraced this approach to litigation and the representation of my clients became a personal struggle with the goal of winning over the lawyers on the other side of the case on every issue and at all costs. Generally, losing a small battle during the course of a protracted litigation resulted in anger, animosity and a desire for revenge against the lawyer on the other side who had handed me defeat. Winning and "getting even" with the lawyers on the other side of the case became an obsession in my work. I believed that it was necessary to be strongly and personally emotionally driven in order to secure victory on behalf of my client. This attitude and behavior naturally resulted in a tremendous amount of stress, emotional ups and downs and periodic depressions. I dealt with these ups and downs in the same way as the lawyers who trained me, including drinking alcohol and other diversions.

After practicing Vipassana I began to see that there was a more balanced way of approaching representation of my clients in litigation. I began to work harder to try and find a middle ground or a compromise solution to settle the controversy between the parties to a litigation. When the matter could not be settled and it was clear that the litigation must proceed to a conclusion, I began to see that the entire process of litigation and the resolution of a conflict between two parties to a lawsuit as a sort of game. It became clear that litigation was a game, which could be played very effectively while still remaining dispassionate and emotionally balanced. I found that I could even more effectively accomplish the goal of furthering my client's interest in a lawsuit by not succumbing to angry reactions to the actions of the other side. By remaining emotionally balanced in the face of aggressive hard ball tactics against me by my opponents in litigation I found that I could speak with even stronger words and still take strong actions. It was much easier to effectively implement the strong actions necessary to tactically and strategically further the best interests of my client without becoming emotionally caught up in the battle itself.

The realization of these truths and the ability to put them into action in my profession are the two key elements that enabled me to continue to practice law after I began meditating. Without the balance and calmness of mind that came to me through my meditation practice, I would have been unable to continue to work as a lawyer. It had become virtually impossible for me to continue to face the difficulties inherent in representing clients who have problems and who are engaged in serious conflicting relationships with other people. Dhamma made it possible again.

My experience with the application of Vipassana to my professional life has helped me understand more deeply the meaning of the phrase "art of living." Without the application of this art to my profession I would have had to change it and do something entirely different for my livelihood.

—*Thomas Crisman, Dallas, USA*

❧

A good teacher lingers in the memory—not for their theorems or drills but for more elusive qualities that catch a spark in us, a love of learning, responsiveness, humor. In their classroom or office we forget schooling and instead we harvest precious lessons for life.

Guy Dubois, a schoolteacher from France, presented his particular professional experience to a Vipassana seminar at Dhamma Giri, India.

I have been meditating for almost six years now and would like to give a glimpse of some of the benefits that I have gradually gained, regarding my activities as teacher and educator.

Nine years ago I began to teach with all the enthusiasm and good will of my youth. But within a short time, I realized that even these qualities and all my scholastic knowledge only gave me superficial fulfillment.

In the East, discipline and respect for the teacher still exist. In my country France, if the teacher is not more interesting than the television, the students soon become restless and challenging, making him uncomfortably aware of his own shortcomings.

When this occurs and when the enthusiasm fades away, quite often he will respond negatively and subjectively. As a consequence, in order to protect himself, a teacher might build a wall of defence, making his teaching distant, cold, strict and academic, producing a lifeless routine in the classroom. Alternatively, he might become overwhelmed, which could lead to smoking, drinking, tranquillizers and sleeping pills, even a nervous breakdown. In France we have psychiatric clinics especially for teachers who cannot cope with the stress of teaching.

For my part, instead of finding fault in others, I was sincerely determined to solve the problem at its roots; and my quest finally brought me to Vipassana.

Within my first meditation course many realities became clearer; my suffering was more bitter than I could ever imagine. Even with my genuine goodwill to help by teaching, I was still unknowingly throwing my inner conflicts on pupils, compensating for past frustrations and inferiority complexes by various games of my ego. So, out of fear of being overpowered, I was trying to manipulate, to control students, either through knowledge or by authoritarian blind reactions.

Also I could not admit in front of others when I was wrong or ignorant. Totally engaged in making shows or fearful of being hurt, I was only able to give attention to and really know the pupils who either pleased me by their brightness or those who made a lot of disturbance.

But by serious practice of Vipassana, my ability to be aware of the habit patterns of my mind, and their manifestation on my body through sensations, has increased as well as my patient acceptance of them. So naturally my stress has been diminishing and my behavior changing.

And now it's like my eyes have been opened. In every successful student, I see also their underlying suffering. In the anonymous, silent ones, I discover their inner qualities. Towards the naughty ones, because I recognize the same misery in me, deeper understanding and tolerance radiate. Whenever I am overwhelmed by negativities, I try to feel these unpleasant sensations with a balanced mind and very soon my irritation decreases. But if I have to take strong action, I have the courage to carry it out, aware that my role is to help rather than please.

By feeling less superior, the atmosphere in the classroom changes. Greater confidence between myself and the students is established, which opens their minds to more difficult topics and increases my sensitivity to problem areas. My words and deeds naturally get strengthened. My ability to communicate effectively expands, not only with the limited intellectual mind, but from the totality of one human being to another equal human being. Here the real exchange starts, where we give and receive on both sides.

You ask what I do. Well, I'm a teacher. I teach in a community college near Seattle and I work with international students as a teacher of English as a second language (ESL). That's a surface view of my job, but underneath it's more about language as a vehicle of communication. I'm hopefully enabling people to communicate better with one another so that the end result will be a more harmonious environment in which people can interact.

I've chosen an international group of people to work with, because I feel it's critical for people to be able to interact internationally. Some success has come from that. Here's an example. During this last year I was working on a special contract in an electronics company and a large percentage of the workers there were from Southeast Asia. They'd been there working in this company for a long time—8, 10, 15 years—and still they weren't talking to the native English speakers in the company. They would work together but they wouldn't talk. So I developed a program where I was hired to teach ESL. I said, "No, I'm going to teach communication skills, and I want these Americans coming into this class as well. I don't want only these non-native speakers." And we sat them down together and we gave them some things to do together. And they came out afterwards saying, "I've never talked to this person before, now I talked to them in the hall." This is what I do. I'm teaching language, but I'm teaching it as a vehicle for people to interact on more than just a "Hi, how're you doing?" level.

I apply Vipassana in my work all the time. For me Vipassana is a way of finding out the truth of the matter. It's always with me because, as much as possible, I'm aware of the truth within. Being aware of sensations. Being aware of the breath. Being aware of how that's manifesting. Being aware of bringing into my interactions that quality of understanding, of wisdom, of compassion, of *mettā*. And so, as much as I possibly can, that's what I try to infuse my work with as a teacher. The most important thing for me as an instructor, which is my chosen profession, is to model what I understand to be the truth in the best possible way I can. That will impact the students—has; continues to; and I keep working to perfect it.

—*In conversation, Peter Martin, who lives and works in Washington, USA*

At times, as a counsellor, I have to deal with violent students and situations. One situation comes to my mind. A 13 year old student, I will call him John, has attended our school since Kindergarten. Usually he is a pleasant and polite boy, but when he gets angry he is at times almost uncontrollable. Although John still has difficulties, he has improved greatly over the years. Many times he will come to me to tell me how angry he is with another child, but through talking it out he is able to settle these differences peacefully. There is still the rare occasion where I have had to restrain him physically and, as he is quite big and powerful for his age, may actually have to sit on him until he calms down. John comes from an environment where problems are often solved by violence. This year I was helping to teach a class with a guest speaker, when John and another boy had a misunderstanding. Before anyone knew what was happening, John pulled this boy from his seat onto the floor and was punching him. I needed to restrain John physically and push him out of the room. I took him to my office and spoke to him quietly. After a fair amount of time, he had calmed down enough to speak with the other boy. Apologies were made and in the end they worked out their differences enough that they actually were friends for the rest of the school year. In addition, John wrote a letter of apology to our guest.

Throughout this episode I tried to use what I had learned through Vipassana to handle the situation. I stayed calm and did not get angry even though I did have to act quickly and strongly. When talking with John I felt my *mettā*, expressed as caring and concern, helped him calm down and feel less defensive. He was then willing to look at and admit what he had done wrong and to take appropriate action to make up for the situation. I was able to help both boys come to a mutually satisfying understanding by not reacting, but by looking at the situation clearly and calmly.

Fortunately this extreme situation is rare. At the same time, it is common for me to have to sit with children or their families when a tragedy has occurred; the death of a grandparent or parent, or a separation in the family. At times, when there is not much to say, I find myself sitting quietly with the child, sending *mettā*. He or she tells me, as they leave my office, that though they still feel sad they are more at peace.

—*Sheldon Klein is an elementary school counsellor in Canada. Both he and his wife practice Vipassana.*

The Buddha has been described as "The Great Physician" for his unique prescription to end human suffering. Meditation, by healing the healer, enhances substantively the quality of care given to the sick in our communities.

Dr Om Prakash, one of the leading doctors in Burma, later moved to Delhi, India, where he continued his professional work including service at free clinics, into his 80s.

Vipassana helps a lot in the practice of medicine. I was quite young when I started practicing Vipassana. At that time I was living in Burma and had a flourishing practice, seeing 250 to 300 patients every day. On entering the clinic I used to be excited and agitated, wondering how I could see so many patients and how I could finish my work in time. I often used to lose my temper, would get angry at the nurse, and would shout at my assistant.

But as I started practicing Vipassana I saw that I was able to work without losing my peace of mind. My medical practice grew, but I no longer felt agitated. My attitude towards my problems changed. Initially, I used to think about the patient's ability to pay for my treatment. After Vipassana, I started thinking: "Oh, what would I do if my son or grandson became sick. This child is like my grandson!" I found that now I had nothing but compassion and loving kindness for my patients.

I also found that my treatments became more effective and beneficial. I was giving the same medicines, but the results were far better. The patients would become well more quickly, even though I was giving the same medicines! In fact, I was using smaller quantities, so people would ask if I was giving them homeopathic medicines, and why I was not giving them modern conventional medicines.

I realized that the medicines I gave were less important than my compassion and *mettā*. Patients started getting cured no matter what medicine I prescribed. Thus the professional can benefit from Vipassana and help people.

I didn't become a physician until a number of years after I had started practicing Vipassana. But it's such a support in the profession. One of the things that I notice is that in any helping profession you're working with people, you're constantly surrounded by people that are sick. They're really suffering in a very obvious way: they're scared, they're in pain, they're often angry, they often feel ripped off and bitter and twisted: "Why is this happening to me!" Or they're angry because they're trying to cover up guilt or fear about what's going on. They're losing control and you're surrounded by this all the time. It's very hard not to get pulled into it or for thoughts to go through your head. For example, say a patient comes in and starts telling me about their drug problem or their alcohol problem. Little thoughts might come in there, contempt for the person, like, "Oh get your act together!" Then maybe they even get abusive, that happens quite often, they throw their anger at you.

The more you do Vipassana, the more you become aware of your own reactions and you just come back to your sensations for a minute and all this defensiveness and ego comes up like, "How dare this person treat me like that, I'm trying to help them!" And it's just enough sometimes. Sometimes you make the wrong choice and you react and you lash out at them. But sometimes it's enough to kind of calm it down so you can get past your own ego and say, "God this guy is really hurting—let me see what I can do to help him." And sometimes you succeed and sometimes you fail but the process really works. It also helps if you're being pulled down by a depressed person and you start to feel down and helpless like, "How am I going to help, I don't see what I can do . . . ." You just try to come back to this base of balance or equanimity, get out of your own attachment to having to be the hero and having to help everybody and fix everything and just be there for the person. People seem to get aligned with that, it helps them and it certainly prevents you from being sucked in.

—*Lemay Henderson sat her first Vipassana retreat in USA in 1985. All her family have since taken courses.*

❧

Geo Poland from Canada recently returned to medical practice after giving longtime service to Vipassana around the world.

Many years ago I struck up a deep friendship with an 85 year old crippled farmer patient of mine. We would while away the hours in his kitchen drinking tea and swapping stories. He was a very practical man who had been successful at almost everything he did. He told me that he only went to school for one day and learned all he needed to know. The teacher wrote on the board "Never Be Idle," so he went back to the farm and started working!

He also told me that in the good old days he had had a doctor who was a real doctor. He said the moment you entered his office you started feeling better, and by the time you left his office you felt even more relieved although you hadn't yet taken any medicine. He then explained that it is very easy to be a good doctor—all you need to do is give the patients lots of "TLC" (tender loving care). Certainly this is not all there is to the practice of medicine, but it is a part which is gradually being replaced by our dependence on investigations, tests and so on to make the diagnosis.

Through Vipassana and the development of *mettā*, we can rekindle this TLC. "Physician heal thyself" is a well known phrase. We of the healing professions should take this to heart if we really want to help ourselves and likewise our patients.

Power For Good

Politicians and administrators hold some of the most powerful positions in society, with the potential for affecting the lives of huge populations. But, as we know, together with power goes temptation—the almost irresistible temptation to abuse office and public trust for their own ends, financial, sexual, dynastic and so on. Undertaking such responsibilities and carrying them out humanely, efficiently, and with integrity is rare indeed. Using one's own vision and strength of character to transform institutions for the selfless benefit of others requires special qualities. A very few individuals, Gandhi, Mandela, Mother Theresa, seem to be born to lead in this unique way. But whatever our starting point, the process of self-introspection and purification of mind through Vipassana, offers all of us a chance of lifetime learning, creative participation, and of realizing the very best in us.

Despite the handicap of poverty and lack of higher education, U Ba Khin made his way professionally. He won admiration for his honesty, intelligence and willingness to work hard. From being a junior clerk in the colonial administration, he rose in 1948 to become the first Accountant General of the newly independent government of Burma. By that time he had already been practicing Vipassana meditation for over ten years. He made rapid progress on the path and began to teach the technique when work duties allowed. For the next two decades he combined the responsibilities of serving his country as a high-ranking civil servant, with those of a lay meditation teacher, producing outstanding results in both fields and earning for himself the title "Sayagyi"—respected teacher.

U Ba Khin was both a man of principle and extremely practical in dealing with people. He could be soft as a rose petal or hard as a diamond, as the situation required. By introducing the practice of Vipassana to the officers and staff of the Accountant General's office, U Ba Khin brought about remarkable improvements in that government department. The Prime Minister recognized the scale of this achievement and wanted an honest administration. So he personally assigned Sayagyi to work with the State Agriculture Marketing Board, one of the most important government offices, which was in poor shape. The report of the committee of enquiry investigating the affairs of the Board unflinchingly exposed a net of corruption and inefficiency. To reform the Board, it would be necessary to override the opposition of the traders and politicians involved. When it was announced that U Ba Khin was to be appointed Chairman of the Board, all the executive officers in the department went on strike, fearful that the man who had exposed their malpractices and inefficiencies was now to become their superior. Sayagyi remained firm. He continued the work of administration with just the clerical staff. After several weeks the strikers, comprehending that Sayagyi was not going to submit to their pressure, capitulated unconditionally and returned to their posts.

Having established his authority, Sayagyi then began, with great love and compassion, to change the entire atmosphere of the Board and its workings. Many of the officers actually joined Vipassana courses under his guidance. In the two years that Sayagyi held the Chairmanship, the Board attained record levels in export and profit and efficiency reached an all-time high.

—from the Sayagyi U Ba Khin Journal

After several years working as an economic policy analyst and adviser in the UK, I found that my work began to suffer from problems in my personal life. I decided to leave the job and resolve my difficulties. I learned the technique of Vipassana during my travels and have continued to practice since 1972.

Meditation has brought major changes in the direction of my life. In 1984, settled in Australia with a wife and two children, I decided to return to economics after a gap of nearly twelve years. From initial research work for the State of Queensland, I was soon involved in Cabinet meetings and strategic decision-making.

The practice of Vipassana has contributed to my working life in many ways. It has provided a psychological and temperamental basis for dealing with major policy issues and leaders of society, often under extreme pressure. It has helped me to see clearly the essence of a problem, and to maintain sustained effort as required. It has also provided a basis for contributing to the morale and wellbeing of my fellow workers.

—Martin Clarke is a senior economist and
government adviser in Australia.

Reluctantly the Home Secretary for the State of Rajasthan (India), agreed to accompany his wife on a Vipassana retreat. He was amazed at the result, not only at the joy and new hope in his wife's face, but at the benefits he himself felt and the realization that in just ten days one could learn a technique which had unlimited possibilities for self improvement. In the area of education and training, attempts were ongoing worldwide to devise a technique which can bring about changes in people's attitude. Ways of imparting information, knowledge and skills had been greatly refined but no reliable method had been found which can transform the human mind and human behavior. Vipassana, he realized, could have a major impact on government through attitude change.

The State government took a pioneering decision to introduce Vipassana as a means of reform in its own organizations. Courses attended by both prisoners and staff were arranged in jail and the police academy also hosted a course, both demonstrating a significant impact on the participants. During the same period, some senior officer meditators in the Home Department were instrumental in initiating internal reforms leading to the reduction of paperwork, quicker decision-making, the clearance of years' work backlog and better staff-officer relationships. In 1977 the Rajasthan State government leased very suitable land outside the majestic city of Jaipur for the construction of a Vipassana center—Dhamma Thali. The success of these initiatives showed what could be done in the direction of change and reform in government through Vipassana. Many states have now taken up the Government of India's recommendation to introduce Vipassana in prisons as a reform measure. A number of states also offer paid leave to civil servants so that they can attend a retreat. The experience of a Vipassana course is being incorporated into some training programs in the police service, for business and technology graduates, for the next generation's high-flying administrators.

Two thousand years before, the Great Emperor Aśoka, a ruler to rival Caesar or Charlemagne, had shown the way. Renouncing the cruelty of conquest for which he was known, he dedicated himself to the welfare of his people. Leading by example, encouraging the populace to take up meditation, he used Vipassana as an instrument of reform in the governance of his vast empire. The record of his administration, chiselled on pillars and rocks, remains to this day. High aspirations and management skills alone cannot bring about good government. Attitudes have to change—a timeless challenge to humankind. Vipassana can, and does, change attitudes.

—Ram Singh, Rajasthan State Home Secretary
during the 1970s, lives in Jaipur
with his wife and family.

Chapter 11

ONE TRUTH—VIPASSANA, SCIENCE AND SPIRITUALITY

The day's sitting came to an end. I went out to the garden. There were already plenty of dewdrops on the grass, a sky full of stars was twinkling and sparkling. The Milky Way was clear in sight, Cassiopeia, Pleiades, Cygnus and other constellations were traced. I realised through the whirl of sensations I was feeling that my body was void and gaseous just like this spacious sky where countless stars were sparkling and moving so rapidly. My body felt solid and tangible, but the fact was that it was gaseous and empty. It might be mine and it might not. Who was this I? Suddenly it occurred to me that I had always been so selfish and egotistical up until this moment. Tears rolled down my cheeks, I cried out loud , not for sorrow but for inexplicable joy. At least at that moment I was humble enough to thank everyone and everything.

Lying down on a log bench, I looked up at the sky again. The whole universe was a vivid organic entity now, I could even sense it was revolving very slowly. The starry sky up there and the starry universe inside of me that I glimpsed a short while ago in meditation were beautifully resonating. I felt so assured and secure, happy and content.

—Yohtaro Ota recalls this incident from his first ten-day course in 1992. An acupuncturist, he later translated The Art of Living *into his native Japanese.*

Vipassana is not a religion, yet the process of introspection, exploration of the truth inside ourselves and outside in the world, is certainly religious. The meditation practice helps us understand the purpose of life and how it should be lived. Above all it provides us with a practical tool for attaining the highest goals of which we are capable.

Vipassana is a universal technique, open to all, practiced by all, benefiting all irrespective of religious or cultural background, nationality, gender or class. The Buddha, a real historical figure, discovered and taught Vipassana, compassionately distributing the teaching freely far and wide. The term "Buddhist," never used by him, only came into existence some centuries later. The Buddha himself referred to the teaching simply as "Dhamma"—the timeless law of nature, the truth, which anyone can realize for themselves. He repeatedly emphasized the personal nature of the quest for enlightenment and the work involved. The results will come from your own practice, he explained, not through dependence on a teacher, blind faith or establishing a sect. Over time organized religions tend to degenerate into sectarianism, dividing people, even turning them against each other, rather than underlining their common humanity and uniting them. "Dhamma," as taught by the Buddha, is always inclusive and never the monopoly of one group or sect.

I've always been of the opinion that there is more to life than what appears in most Western societies to be important. While needing basics to live, I have always doubted my own need, or desire, to compete. Despite many interests, I always felt "unambitious" in any conventional sense. I'd always felt more complete being creative for its own sake, enjoying deep conversations or simply being at one with nature, in forests, mountains or by the sea.

In terms of a career, I trained and qualified as a lawyer in 1992, but left disillusioned. Little did I suspect that my sense of dissatisfaction was an underlying truth of the Buddha's teaching.

The 1980s had convinced me that I needed some sort of healing, some more profound spiritual depth in my life. Like many Westerners though, it never really occurred to me to seek this in organized religion. My own parents are neither strongly for nor against, so in that sense I never railed against religion—it merely seemed to lack depth or sincerity for me.

After a period of confusion and loss of direction, I managed to take the plunge in a new direction, and began art classes, in the hope of somehow harnessing the ability I felt I had in that area. This culminated in a further degree, but again I found myself with more questions than answers. Surprise, surprise, more unsatisfactoriness.

—Robert Hider lives in UK with his wife, a comeditator, and daughter and works as a printmaker, organic farmer and artist.
"I've found the path I'd been waiting unknowingly for since I don't know when," he wrote a year after practicing Vipassana.

Applied Science

"Dhamma" and "science" are frequently pitted against one another. Actually they represent two complementary aspects of human activity. We are an inquisitive species, always wanting to know and understand ourselves and the world. Right from birth, a child tries to figure out the cause-effect relationship among various events around them: pushing a switch lights a bulb, putting ice in a glass of soft drink cools it. Science synthesizes all the knowledge that we have gained about the external world, with the help of our senses.

As the child grows into maturity and experiences life's ups and downs, he or she often begins to question: "What is the point of all this—being born, studying, earning, having children, raising a family, retirement and finally dying? Why is there so much suffering, caused by illness, old age, separation from loved ones, association with undesirables?" They begin to consider the real cause of their suffering and the way out of it and thus become wiser. Dhamma synthesizes all the wisdom gained by humanity; it reveals the laws relating to our inner world, just as science deals with the laws pertaining to the outside world.

For the harmonious development of individuals and society, proper integration of science and Dhamma is essential, yet they are often perceived as irreconcilable. Dhamma for many people today has become identified with sectarian religions, ritual, community conflicts and a stubborn resistance to any logical scrutiny of beliefs. Science meanwhile is usually associated with thoroughgoing materialism—the view that matter is the only reality.

Vipassana uses a scientific approach to probe the truth inside. The meditation technique enables anyone to experience the laws of nature, not just a select few. Every proposition is presented as a hypothesis to be accepted only on verification by experience and not on authority. Although spiritual experience is by definition personal, it can be shared and verified in the personal experience of others. Such propositions must also prove rational and logical to be acceptable.

It has long been recognized that the ability to cap sense desires is an important human attainment. But if we are not to simply give way to the urge to express anger and passion, how do we avoid suppressing these emotions in the subconscious when we divert our attention?

Vipassana offers a method for purifying the mind of its baser instincts. Step by step we can learn to identify these mental defilements objectively and by detached observation within the mental-physical structure we can eliminate them. Working with the natural breath and body sensations, the technique can be easily understood and the results immediately verified by personal experience. It is an applied science, a technology for inner development, no prior belief is necessary to undertake the meditation and like every technical skill it can be accomplished by anyone through systematic practice.

Historically the rise of science encouraged the materialistic belief that all phenomena could be explained rationally on the basis of well understood laws of nature. In the West, mind and matter were seen as separate entities, mind's perceived subjectivity making it the poor relation. Even today any suggestion about "transcending the intellect" is often seen as unscientific. However recent developments in science such as the theory of relativity and quantum mechanics are bringing about a profound change in our accepted view of nature. The truths of impermanence and egolessness in the universe, the interconnectedness of mind with matter, are being discovered in fields as diverse as physics, biology, psychology and neuroscience. The emerging world view recognizes the role of direct experience or insight alongside traditional approaches to understanding "reality." Beyond apparent contradictions, the perspectives of Dhamma and science complement one another, vastly enhancing our understanding and showing us wise ways forward.

Long before the discoveries of modern science, the Buddha realized by examining himself in deep meditation that the entire material structure is composed of minute subatomic particles, which arise and vanish trillions of times in the blink of an eye. Some years ago an American scientist received the Nobel Prize in Physics. He had devised an instrument, a bubble chamber, capable of calculating how rapidly particles in the universe change. He found that in one second a subatomic particle arises and vanishes 10^{22} times. The two "scientists" came to the same conclusion. But whereas the Buddha experienced the truth directly for himself, the physicist relied for information on his instrument and intellectual wisdom only. The Buddha attained liberation from all suffering through his research. Did the Nobel Prize winner likewise gain enlightenment?

—*S.N. Goenka, edited story from a ten-day discourse.*

&

What is happiness? For all that science has achieved in the field of materialism, are the peoples of the world happy? They may find sensual pleasures off and on, but in their heart of hearts, they are not happy when they realize what has happened, what is happening and what may happen next. Why? This is because, while man has mastery over matter, he is still lacking in mastery over his mind.

Instead of using intelligence for the conquest of atomic energy in matter without, why not use it also for the conquest of atomic energy within. This will give us the "Peace within" and will enable us to share it with all others.

—*Sayagyi U Ba Khin, Vipassana Teacher*

Universal Teaching

Vipassana is a universal technique. It confronts the common human problem of suffering and addresses the common human need for consolation—relief from sorrow. Meditation courses have been organized in Christian churches and seminaries, a Muslim mosque, Hindu and Buddhist religious places. Thousands of followers of the various world religions and many of their leaders are taking Vipassana courses. Atheists and agnostics are also attracted. Why?

The mental training we undertake practicing Vipassana—morality, concentration and purification of mind—is entirely nondenominational. The objects of meditation, breath and body sensations, have no sectarian association. Religious conversion is not involved. One can remain within one's religion or tradition and still gain all the benefits of meditation. Confidence or faith is an invaluable support on the path. But faith needs to be properly founded on wholesome qualities in people, gods, religion which inspire us to improve ourselves. No one can do that for us; we must understand that only we can do the work and experience the results now and in future. The common task is to become a better human being. Whatever our background, if we accept this responsibility, Vipassana will take us towards the goal.

Most people in the West come from Christian backgrounds. For some it is part of their upbringing and culture which remains more or less buried, rejected even. Others however, everyday folk as well as nuns, monks and priests, maintain an active faith. Vipassana helps us reconnect with our spiritual roots and through the direct experience of truth in meditation grow as individuals.

Bill Vorhauer was engaged for much of his professional life as an educator and social worker in Hispanic communities within the United States. Now retired, he intends to spend more time sitting and serving at Vipassana centers and maybe constructing some straw bale buildings.

"Most men lead lives of quiet desperation." H.D. Thoreau

" . . . is it weakness of intellect birdie, I cried,
or a rather tough worm in your little inside?"

Gilbert & Sullivan

At 3:00 in the morning of a sleepless night, when the brain begins to buzz like a bad fluorescent light, I used to wonder what all the fuss and feathers of the day were all about. Or if it had been a placid day, had I wasted it by not being in the thick of the daily battle to get something done in the bureaucracy? And anyway, was this or that more worthwhile, or was the whole thing a self deception?

The struggle to get one's point, sales quota, or promotion; wasn't there anything better to draw breath for, let alone live or die for? Never mind the high drama, all I ever wanted was just a tad of conviction or a subjective reality instead of always feeling poised precariously on a ball bearing platform just the size of my footprint.

"You don't know what a poor opinion I have of myself, and how little I deserve it." Gilbert & Sullivan

In the U.S., the minorities that buy into the rat race try to outdo what the mainstream white person achieves due to the lack of artificial barriers. His own group will accuse him of assimilationism and the others will not care at all, or if they do it will be to make invidious comments. As a Mexican-American, I found myself lost in this morass in spite of the fact that I had sought affiliation through a very active pentecostal participation since I was 14. At 16, I converted my parents and we all became Mennonites (Anabaptists). At 18, organized religion lost all appeal for me.

Up until my 53rd year, I worked and prayed for some sense of certainty or satisfaction because it appeared that the people that I knew seemed satisfied with the goals and rewards of ordinary life and pursued them avidly: fishing, jet skiing, spectator sports, beer, bar hopping and all. I think I would have been a dedicated alcoholic if the hangovers weren't so vicious. So there it is in a nutshell: the gnawing worm in the mind, the feeling of alienation, and no source of peace or satisfaction.

In 1978, when I first learned about Vipassana, two major realizations changed the landscape of my mind. After so many years of uncertainty and confusion, I had finally found a subjective reality that required no faith or proof outside of myself.

Upon careful repeated examination of all my hopes, desires and wants, it finally dawned on me that my conditioned desires were the root cause of my mental misery. In my ignorance (actively conditioned and manipulated by every element of society) I had sought comfort, assurance and security in things and the standard program of family life. When this became a self-verified, incontrovertible conclusion I felt that I had been released from prison and was breathing new air. Elated is too mild a word to express my newfound state of mind.

The second part of my new subjective reality (and I urge an understanding of what the operative effects are of a subjective reality) was that I had believed an untruth. I now had the means to disabuse myself of the notion that I had ever been in control of my mind. Through Vipassana it had become abundantly clear that the usual state of anyone's mind is one of chaos: I was on one end of the rope and the wild horse of my mind was on the other end and I was daily being dragged through thorns, mud, muck and rocky ground and my standard was how much or how little skin I had lost that day. It was as if I thought being dragged was the normal mode of transportation.

It might be said that Vipassana held out the knowledge of saddles and horsemanship. There was the hope or faith that issues from no other alternative. There was also the perfect understanding and experience of many meditators to bolster my confidence that mental horsemanship was a skill like any other and although it might be simple, it was neither easy nor quick after fifty-three years of running wild, but nevertheless possible and probable through sufficient practice. It is never too late unless you don't start.

&

Father Desmond D'Souza, a Redemptionist retreat teacher for over a quarter century and ex-secretary to the Third World Protestant Churches in Singapore, likened attending a ten-day course to a second deeper training for his vocation.

Vipassana represents a radical shift from a deductive, theoretical, prefabricated system to an inductive, experiential way of learning. No book, no Bible, no rosary, no mass, no prayer, no God—nothing. You go empty. And there you begin to find that the "real" book is yourself, your own body and mind. You discover that within yourself there are laws operating which are the same laws operating in the universe outside . . . .

So now I am not starting any more from a system of beliefs—I am not starting from my belief in God. I am starting from Jesus of Nazareth, a human being going through a similar process of purification towards an enlightenment that ultimately was transformed by God. Vipassana is the best process of acquired contemplation. We can come to the highest state of sensitivity to receive the gift of God's grace.

&

Father John Chang sat his first course in Taiwan before being assigned to work in Brazil.

Vipassana serves as my daily spiritual practice. It provides me with the strength and power to respond to the demands of my ministry as a Catholic priest. It helps me to have a clear and open view about religious practices. It inspires me to have a better understanding of the teachings of Jesus and the books in the Bible. With the practical perspective of Vipassana, the words of Jesus recorded in the Bible make sense to me. The words become alive. It is no longer simply the authority of the Bible but the authority that comes from sharing the same wisdom about life. It delights me to see that Buddha and Jesus are sharing the same wisdom in the art of living. Vipassana also helps me to have better control over my mind and sets me free more quickly from sad and undelightful moments. It helps my understanding of the human weakness of others and gives me more compassion towards the needy.

Fundamentalism, conservatism, exclusiveness, narrow-mindedness, prejudice—all encountered within my religious circle—can be reviewed and reduced through Vipassana. Jesus said "The truth will set you free." The power of Vipassana can help people to see the truth themselves, the very act of seeing will set them free from the bondage of ignorance and delusion. Vipassana creates light with which to see and catch the essentials of religion, reduces gaps and conflicts, and encourages the religiously minded to look for the common good and the improved welfare of the entire universe. In other words, it provides a new horizon and vision of life.

Muslims are sometimes reticent to take up meditation because they fear it might be in conflict with their religious principles. However a respected religious scholar recently commented in the Arab News that if meditation requires no particular ritual then what is desirable and encouraged by Islam can be achieved through introspection. Many Muslims from different schools and communities have discovered in Vipassana a technique which enhances their lives as Muslims while in no way requiring them to identify themselves with the practice of some other religion.

Despite the sincere recommendation of a friend, Mohammed Arif Joyia hesitated about taking a course:

"Oh! This is the religion of Buddhists, atheists. These Buddhists don't believe in Soul and God. What can they teach? I am a Muslim. I cannot commit this crime." Overcoming these fears he decided to join the course (Hyderabad, India—1978) and made good progress. However one night while sleeping he suddenly saw a ferocious demon, which seized him by the neck and threatened him for coming to the meditation center. Waking in a fright, Mohammed saw his roommates peacefully sleeping and realized that it was a nightmare, a play of the mind, impurities shaken by serious meditation being eradicated. "I now understood. This is a conspiracy of the unconscious mind. I am not leaving without completing the course." He relaxed, smilingly returned to bed and eventually fell asleep.

Next day, feeling calm and detached, Mohammed found a fresh perspective on his experience: "I now understood the meaning of 'I take refuge in Buddha' as refuge in one's own enlightenment, not the personality of Siddhartha Gotama. The meaning of 'I take refuge in Dhamma' is that one has to be established in one's own true nature, not in any sectarian religion. The meaning of 'I take refuge in Sangha' is to take refuge in those noble ones who have become well established in Dhamma, whatever their race, color or nationality. From this sacred moment onwards, the word death, full of theories and tears, just flowed away like melted snow. Oh, no! No being dies. Death is impossible. Everyone keeps on moving on the journey according to one's own actions. And the final destination of the journey is *nibbāna*. Now I understood what one's own religion is and what the religion of others is. Without purifying the mind by Vipassana and realizing our own nature, life is lived in the religion of others. Living in one's own nature is the true Dhamma."

Later Mohammed wrote: "I would like to tell all my young educated Muslims that they should really try Vipassana and see the results. It is a necessity today that people of all different walks of life unite." In fact worldwide Muslims are being attracted to Vipassana in growing numbers; retreats have been held in several Gulf States and "The Art of Living" has been approved and published in the Farsi language.

After fifteen years having studied, experienced and taught different methods of meditation, I came across the technique taught by Mr. Goenka and found it very effective. I was a yoga teacher for many years and have trained many students. I have also written a book on the subject of yoga and meditation. But with Vipassana—as Mr Goenka teaches it—I completed the last of my experiments.

As an Iranian, familiar with the profound teachings of Eastern mysticism, I have spent my life aspiring beyond materialism and I have witnessed that this impermanent world is a shadow to the ultimate truth. I found in Mr. Goenka's words a deep mutual understanding; I believed the Buddha's teaching and appreciated through experience the effectiveness of this method of meditation.

—*Dr Ahmad Nourbaksh is a university teacher*
in Teheran, Iran.

Throughout the Jewish diaspora many are enthusiastically practicing Vipassana, particularly in Israel where courses are regularly given and usually oversubscribed.

Paul Glantz, a 33 year old Jewish rabbi, attended a Vipassana course in Sussex, England during one holiday and wrote about it for his synagogue bulletin.

I did think to myself on more than one occasion, "Why am I here?" but it was a pleasure not to have to talk or even acknowledge anyone else. I often wanted to suddenly burst into song in the dining room. But I kept to the rules and did not say any other rituals, prayers or even chat to God because a deal is a deal.

The idea is that the meditation and this style of living cleanses one of all the tensions which we store in our bodies. Every evening there was video about the theory behind the technique and in this it was explained that cravings and aversions are the roots of all our problems; that we want things to happen and we want to avoid other things happening. The meditation is meant to retrain the mind not to react to either our cravings or aversions. It was fascinating for me to reconsider the Jewish idea of *Yetzer Ha-Ra*, the bad inclination, which is so similar to this. The early rabbis, according to the Mishna, would meditate for hours before they prayed. We do not know what technique they used but for me this meditation technique seems very applicable. The retreat gave me a splendid opportunity to start to cleanse myself physically and emotionally before Yom Kippur. I would even consider doing it again next year!

India is renowned for spirituality, with its wealth of gods, religious practices and meditation techniques. Vipassana originated here and has revived rapidly across the country in recent years. However the hold of tradition remains strong, particularly among older generations, and sometimes it takes some special impetus to propel individuals towards a fresh perspective and personal change.

1984 was a particularly difficult year for all sensitive people in India. Operation Bluestar in the Punjab resulted in massive bloodshed at a much revered Sikh temple. The Prime Minister, Mrs Gandhi was assassinated, which was followed by terrible riots across the north of the country. Then, as if that wasn't sorrow enough for the country, the industrial disaster at the chemical plant in Bhopal killed and injured thousands. For PL Dhar, a university teacher at the Institute of Technology, Delhi, all these events were overshadowed by the unexpected illness and death of his eldest son.

From college days Dhar showed a spiritual inclination. He began regular study of the Hindu classics such as *Bhagavad-Gita*, the *Upanishads* and the *Vedas*. He tried various kinds of meditation, mostly through instructions given in books. For a period he became very close to a teacher whose explanations of the scriptures were particularly inspiring.

At an intellectual level, Dhar could understand his son's passing as part of some "divine play" and accept it with composure. However as the months went by, the veneer of equanimity began to wear thin. He felt a strange uneasiness deep inside and found it difficult even to keep up his normal work routine. Perhaps it was true, as he'd heard said, that traditional spiritual practices such as chanting, devotional prayers and thought observation were unable to penetrate into the deeper recesses of the mind. After all there was no reason to be upset and yet he found himself in turmoil. "Where's the need?" he'd replied some months before to a friend's invitation to try a Vipassana retreat. Now the need had made itself known.

The first course was a very difficult experience, not because of long hours of sitting or enforcement of silence; it was the evening discourses that were very difficult to tolerate. These discourses challenged my cherished beliefs and seemed to be making snide and derogatory comments about some of the most revered saints of the past. I confronted Goenkaji, who was himself conducting the course, with my objections. Not feeling satisfied with his response, and with the discourses becoming more and more strident, I even decided to leave the course after the third day. Goenkaji responded very affectionately: "You are a scientist, why not complete the experiment before coming to conclusions? You need not agree to all that is said in the discourse, just practice what is being advised, and then after ten days draw your own conclusions." And thus when he refused to grant permission to go, I said to myself: Why not defer judgment and try to experiment sincerely for the rest of the days. At the end of the course, the effect was evident. I felt so light and happy, as I had never felt in my life.

By the time I was 40, I was a very successful doctor with social status, prestige, a fairly moneyed person having a hospital and house of my own, as well as a loving wife and children. Yet something was missing from my life— the right brain remained unfulfilled. Drawing, painting and musical talent which I had nurtured as a younger man now remained firmly in the background while career and the ambition to succeed, all the left brain achievements, kept getting priority. Inwardly, contentment, happiness, patience, silence, peace and joy were almost unknown in my daily life. I was instead a very impatient, dominant, irritable person whose persistent anger spilled over from my professional into my personal life.

Around this time I came into contact with Osho Rajneesh who advised that to find real happiness and solid values I would have to look within. A new ambition now seized me—the attainment of enlightenment. I was initiated in *sanyas*, wearing red robes and beads. I changed my name and went headlong into various forms of meditation, including a type of *"vipassana."* For several years I practiced in my own way without anyone to guide me, using the teachings of Krishnamurti and others for inspiration. Then by chance I stumbled on a book explaining the technique of Vipassana as taught by S.N. Goenka and realized that what I had been doing was very different. Joining a ten-day course I immediately understood the significance of body sensations in the meditation practice. As a physician treating body and mind for 42 long years, I knew that patients' symptoms were always expressed in terms of body feelings, yet I had never taken the trouble to observe these same sensations in myself. Suddenly I saw myself revealed, always wanting to retain the sensations I loved and be rid of those I hated. My whole existence was governed by sensations. But now at last a way to inner contentment was beckoning—and the key was equanimity . . .

—*Dr HN Phadnis is a Holistic Health counsellor in Pune, India. All members of his extended family practice Vipassana.*

The teachings of the Buddha contain deep inspiration and guidance on how we should conduct ourselves. But devotion towards the Buddha and reading scriptures alone will not bring liberation. His advice was unequivocal, meditate and progress on the path.

When living in Rangoon, Burma I never realized how fortunate I was to be born into a religious family. As in most traditional Buddhist families, performing good deeds such as giving donations and ethical living comes naturally and is part and parcel of our lives. I have also enjoyed the special privileges of being a male Buddhist. I became a novice several times during my teens, and was ordained as a monk after age 20 on several occasions. I had the opportunity to practice *samatha* (concentration) and *vipassanā* (insight)meditation, using different methods at various monasteries and meditation centers. However I never had the chance to meditate at Sayagyi U Ba Khin's center, although it was very close to my wife's home.

On immigrating to the United States and settling down in southern California, my wife, my younger son and I all had a wonderful experience attending the ten-day course at the nearby center. Although assistant teachers led the course, I felt as if Goenkaji himself was conducting it. I was able to appreciate the effectiveness of the use of audio and video teaching materials. I have been to several Vipassana meditation courses in Burma conducted by famous monk-teachers. Most centers there are open throughout the year but they do not conduct a specified course and the teachers themselves may not be available for guidance. At the end of our retreat, I felt very grateful to Goenkaji and to U Ba Khin for their wisdom, foresight and hard work in successfully establishing permanent Vipassana meditation centers around the world.

Although I missed the golden opportunity of participating in Vipassana courses by Sayagyi U Ba Khin himself while residing in Rangoon for forty years, I finally was able to enjoy the fruits of his labors by completing the course at the California center for the first time. For me, it had been "So near and yet so far."

> —*U Tin Htoon sat his first course at Dhamma*
> *Mahāvana, California Vipassana Center in 1996.*
> *He and his family in USA and abroad*
> *continue to meditate in this tradition and stay*
> *in touch with their monk teachers in Myanmar.*

🍃

Angraj Chaudhary is a former Professor of Pāli, the ancient language of India in which the Buddha's teachings are preserved.

I had not actually realized, before I started practicing Vipassana, how fickle my mind is. I had heard about it right enough but I myself had little real understanding. I could speak about its nature glibly to my students when explaining the scriptures but it was only with the experience of Vipassana that I could see just how the mind moves at breakneck speed from one object to another, multiplying our reactions, and fortunately, I could learn to control it. Vipassana has enabled me to understand the Pāli texts better. But most importantly it has helped me grapple more successfully with the storms and volcanoes that lie dormant in myself. The deeper meanings of these verses from the Dhammapada have now become crystal clear:

> The well directed mind, indeed, can do greater good than even one's mother, father and relatives can.

> The ill directed mind, on the other hand, can do greater harm than an enemy does to an enemy, and a hater does to one who hates him.

Reconciling Differing Views

Elevating shared spiritual values over superficial differences, the practice of Vipassana points a way towards genuine understanding and reconciliation within and between diverse faiths and traditions.

The following is an excerpt from a special address titled "Buddha, The Super-Scientist of Peace" given by S.N. Goenka to the United Nations in New York in May 2002.

This is the bold declaration of a supreme scientist. He says, "I have experienced this Law of Nature, the Law of Dependent Origination, within myself; and having experienced and understood it I declare it, teach it, clarify

it, establish it and show it to others. Only after having
seen it for myself, I declare it." Just as whether there is a
Newton or no Newton, the law of gravity remains true.
Newton discovered it and explained it to the world.
Similarly, Galileo or no Galileo, the fact that the earth
revolves around the sun remains true.

The feeling of sensation is the crucial junction from
where one can take two paths going in opposite directions.
If one keeps on reacting blindly to pleasant and unpleasant
sensations, one multiplies one's misery. If one learns to
maintain equanimity in the face of pleasant and unpleasant
sensations, one starts changing the habit pattern at the
deepest level and starts coming out of misery. The
sensations are the root. As long as one neglects the root,
the poisonous tree will grow again even if the trunk is
cut. The Buddha said:

> *Just as a tree with roots intact and secure, though cut down,*
> *sprouts again;*
> *Even so while latent craving is not rooted out, misery*
> *springs up again and again.*

Thus this super-scientist discovered that to become
fully liberated from mental defilements, one has to work
at the root of the mind. Each individual must cut asunder
the roots of craving.

For society to change for the better, the individual has
to change. When the entire forest is withered, each tree
has to be nurtured, its roots cleared of disease, and then
watered. Then the entire forest will bloom again. Similarly,
for the betterment of society, each individual has to
improve. For society to become peaceful, each individual
has to become peaceful. The individual is the key.

Similarly for the world to become peaceful, each
country or society has to become peaceful. Here I would
again like to quote a very important exhortation from
the Buddha to the Vajjian republic of Licchavis. The
Buddha gave the following practical instructions, which
would make the Licchavis unassailable:

- As long as they maintain their unity and meet regularly, they will remain invincible.
- As long as they meet together in unity, rise in unity and perform their duties in unity, they will remain invincible.
- As long as they do not transgress their ancient principles of good governance and their system of justice, they will remain invincible.
- As long as they revere, respect, venerate, and honor their elders and pay regard to their words, they will remain invincible.
- As long as they protect their women and children, they will remain invincible.
- As long as they venerate the objects of worship inside and outside their republic, and maintain monetary support for them, they will remain invincible.

There were many sects in those days too, with their own temples and places of worship. Wisdom lies in keeping all people happy and satisfied. They should not be subjected to harassment, which compels them to become enemies of the state. Their places of worship should receive adequate protection. As long as the rulers provide protection and support to saintly people, they will remain invincible.

This wise counsel by the Buddha is also applicable today to maintain peace and harmony in the world. We cannot ignore issues related to religion if we are to be successful in bringing peace to the world.

It is the duty of every government to protect its people from external attacks, to do everything possible to make its people and territory secure. While this is done, it must be borne in mind that such measures give only short term benefits. Good will and compassion alone can remove the hatred that lies at the root of all such acts performed by anyone belonging to any sect. In India, the United States and other countries where Vipassana courses are held in prisons, we already see how people change. The roots of terrorism lie in the minds of terrorists. We have seen how some hardened, violent criminals have been transformed in our prison courses. Anger, fear, vengefulness and hatred start dissolving, creating a peaceful and compassionate mind. We first ask some members of the prison staff to learn Vipassana and only then give courses for the inmates. This gives wonderful results.

In the Buddha's teaching, we will find a bridge that can connect various sects. The three fundamental divisions of the Buddha's teachings—morality, concentration of mind and purification of mind—are the essence of every religion and spiritual path. *Sīla, samādhi and paññā* are the common denominators of all religions. There can be no conflict over these three basic factors necessary for living a beneficial life. The whole emphasis of the Buddha's teaching is on the practice of these three in order to apply Dhamma in real life. This is the inner core of every religion. Instead of giving importance to this core, we keep on quarreling about the outer shell, which may be different in different religions.

History has proved that whenever the universal, nonsectarian teaching of the Buddha has gone to any place or community, it has never clashed with the traditional culture. Instead, like sugar dissolving in milk, the teachings have been gently assimilated to sweeten and enhance the society. We all know how much the sweetness of peace and tranquillity is needed in the bitter world today. May the teaching of the Enlightened One bring peace and happiness to more and more individuals, thus making more and more societies around the world peaceful and happy.

Chapter 12

COME AND SEE!

I was fortunate to attend a secondary school where apart from the regular subjects we also studied Latin and Greek. We read Plato, Socrates and other philosophers. Something which stuck in my mind was a saying by Heraclitus from Ephesus: *"Panta rei,"* "All things forever flow and change." I did not know why this made such an impression.

At the age of 17 or 18 a friend introduced me to vegetarian food. She also lent me Hesse's book *Siddhartha*, which formed more or less the start of my spiritual search.

The last year of high school we went to Rome with the whole class to visit the places we had heard so much about. Soon after that I also visited Athens with a friend. On the top of the Acropolis I met a German traveller and dental student. We had a lot in common and he told me about meditation for the first time.

After finishing high school I was not sure what to study next. Philosophy was one of the possibilities, it seemed interesting, but I knew I did not really want to learn other people's theories and thoughts, but rather how to live a good life myself. Wisdom was what I was looking for . . . .

—Petra van Domburg is an information technology
trainer in The Netherlands. She has practiced
Vipassana since her first course in 1984.

When Goenkaji started teaching Vipassana in the West in 1979, I was a typical example of a confused and unhappy Westerner in need of his teachings of moderation and wisdom. Like many other young people growing up in the fast-changing sixties and seventies, when the old inequalities of conservative society were being challenged, I had experimented with many conflicting roles and images of myself. I had tried being the quiet student, daughter of humble migrants, fond of classics and crochet. The serious young industrial scientist. The adoring wife, homemaker and gardener. The embroidered-cheesecloth-draped weekend dope-smoker, dreaming of organic farming. The psychedelic astral-traveller. The depressed "tragic victim" of a possessive husband. The leather-clad motorcycle tourer. The blond sun-worshipping Mediterranean nudist. The Himalayan hiker.

None of these roles seemed to fit, so I kept moving from one to another, wanting to be someone else, someone who wasn't me, because I wasn't content with what I was, where I was or what I had. I sometimes tried to be a better and more useful person, but there were so many self-destructive habits that kept me from improving myself.

When a friend at work encouraged me to take a Vipassana course, out of respect for his kindness, I decided to try. It was the hardest thing I had ever done in my life. For once, there was no escape from taking a good close look at myself, and I didn't like very much of what I saw. I was a spoilt and selfish young woman. I had been dishonest and disloyal to my former husband and hurt him very much. There were a few compensating qualities but not many. After the course, I didn't immediately notice any great changes in myself, but there was some sense of hope that it was possible to take control over my life, instead of just reacting to circumstances.

—*Gilly Rowan, Australia*

The search for truth is a very personal journey. An ancient technique of meditation, Vipassana is as relevant now as in the past. The tradition of teaching we have been describing here is distinctive in a number of ways. It is entirely nonsectarian and nonpolitical. Teachers are guides, not gurus. Courses are offered free of charge, funded not from commercial sources but solely through the voluntary donations of grateful students. The approach to meditation is primarily practical; learning how to train and purify the mind to prevail over past conditionings and make a change in our lives for the better. The teaching is simple to understand and follow. On courses as in daily sittings, each element in the training—ethical living, concentration and insight—is essential and supports the others. The direct personal experience of one's own inner reality, mind and body, as it changes moment to moment, is at the core of the practice. Exploring the truth as it is, without recourse to imagination, verbalization or visualization, we will certainly gain good and tangible results from our meditation. Over time our efforts to purify the mind will ripen in the development of qualities of generosity, virtue, patience, self sacrifice, industriousness, truthfulness, determination, compassion, equanimity and wisdom, enabling us to give more to others and hastening our own progress on the path. This then, is an outline of the technique, and how Vipassana meditation can be successfully applied anywhere in the world today.

The initial object of Vipassana meditation is to activate the experience of *anicca* (impermanence) in oneself and to eventually reach a state of inner and outer calmness and balance. This is achieved when one becomes engrossed in the feeling of *anicca* within. The world is now facing serious problems which threaten all mankind. It is just the right time for everyone to take to Vipassana meditation and learn how to find a deep pool of quiet in the midst of all that is happening today. *Anicca* is inside of everybody. It is within reach of everybody. Just a look into oneself and there it is—*anicca* to be experienced . . . . *Anicca* is, for the householder, the gem of life which he will treasure to create a reservoir of balanced energy for his own wellbeing and for the welfare of the society.

—*Sayagyi U Ba Khin*

In meditation you withdraw from others and focus your attention inside to gain purity of mind and Dhamma energy. Then you must become extroverted and use this energy. When you take a long jump, you must first take some steps backward. Then you run, and make the jump. Like this, you first withdraw, observe yourself inside and get the energy. Then you make a long jump into society, to serve society. These two steps cannot be separated.

—*S.N. Goenka*

Silent meditation isn't a way of forgetting but a way of being unable to forget, an instant replay of your own game. Through silent meditation, we cultivate purity not because we want to avoid hell in some afterlife, but because we want to avoid watching ourselves stumble awkwardly across the internal silent screen. A lifelong commitment to this sort of self-awareness naturally purifies life, deleting whatever is incompatible with silent, tranquil peace. The more rigorously we immerse ourselves in ourselves, the nicer a person we're going to want to be. Purity means being able to relax with who we really are. By this I don't mean mere self-acceptance, but self-transformation, so that wherever we penetrate we find no hindrance or harm. We stop shocking ourselves. Meditation focused on purification isn't something we do to overcome our day, but what we do to guide our day toward sustainable peace of heart.

—*from* Cultivating Inner Peace
by Paul Fleischman

Practicing Vipassana helps us face the whirlwind of our lives without fear. We realize change every day by direct experience, processing our internal responses alongside the stream of external happenings. We also realize change by understanding what's true in nature, how this deepest personal reality coexists with surface situations. And we realize change by progressively replacing the reactive instinct with genuine acceptance and positivity. As accounts from real live meditators bear witness, Vipassana is an invaluable tool to solve our problems. Victims no more, working with the grain.

🐘

Charles Brown sat one of the early Vipassana retreats in India, returning to America in 1977 after almost five years away. Both he and the country had altered radically. He had just survived a plane crash in Guatemala (see pp. 8-9) and reentry was tough.

I needed to get some clear space so I borrowed my brother's van which was equipped for sleeping and eating. I went to the eastern side of the mountains where the apple picking season was underway. I got a job in a small orchard where I was the only picker. For two days I was alone picking apples all day and I was alone at night in the camper van. My agitation would not subside, however. Late on the third day I was up a ladder picking apples. Reaching for apple after apple had a hypnotic effect and suddenly a great peacefulness came over me. I sensed that I was back in the crashing airplane and I felt that total calm with which I had faced my death. Then a voice asked me "Completely calm facing your death and now totally upset facing your life?" My unusual reversal of attitudes toward life and death struck me as very amusing. My response would be the exact opposite of almost everyone else in the world. I began to laugh. I began to laugh hard. I was perhaps two meters up the picking ladder and thought I might fall off so I climbed down and continued to laugh on the ground. My laughter shattered the problem. I still had many problems to cope with to bring order back into my life, but the laughter had shattered the one big problem into bite sized chunks. "Remember *anicca*," Goenkaji would say, and here it was come home to me.

> —*Charles Brown recently reconnected with Vipassana after a long layoff in the most unexpected manner. Out of the blue a ten-day course was organized at his place of work, a jail near Seattle. It was the perfect way to pick up his own meditation, and by "taking the practice off the cushion" support the new inmate program at NRF.*

My friend's situation grew worse. He seemed to have tested HIV positive and already have AIDS. He was desperate and the alcohol abuse increased. In the past I would have tried to comfort and help him but I could see that I couldn't help him at all. As they told us at the Al-Anon meetings, you have to learn to detach, to let go by focusing on yourself, changing yourself. Again I tried to help but found myself in one crisis after another. Finally, having lived in this dysfunctional situation for seven years, I felt I couldn't continue and left. I had tried everything, there was nothing more I could do for him.

I went to the Vipassana course to deal with my grief. To my amazement by accepting my present feelings instead of depression, I gained relief. I realized that I can be happy despite the expectation that my dearest friend will die soon. But the surprises didn't end there. I returned home to the news that my friend had been very sick in hospital, where he'd been tested again. He didn't have AIDS, wasn't HIV positive after all.

> —*Werner Jung from Germany is an artist.*

Remember "Eeyore" in Chapter 2 (see p. 11)? Kerry Jacobs from UK keeps ringing the changes.

My mind has become much clearer and quicker, particularly my memory and my ability to arrive quickly at a solution. Recently, when I needed to do some serious revision for a Japanese test to take me up to the next level, I chose to spend more than half of the precious time I had available for revision on attending a ten-day Vipassana course. I wanted to go on the retreat to deepen my meditation, and I wasn't worried about losing ten days of revision because I knew that, if I worked properly, at the end of the course my mind would be so much clearer that it would more than make up for the missed days—and so it did—I passed the test with good marks.

On another occasion, I returned to work after a meditation course to face a problem concerning a computer that had been dragging on for months and months. I began to feel very dispirited and then suddenly thought let's see if we can get to the crux of the matter. I sat down and thought very clearly and deeply about the whole issue for about a minute, realized what I should do and sorted it all out that day. It was quite amazing, and very liberating!

I have also become much more ready to work. My mother used to call me the dormouse, as I was so fond of sleeping when I was little, especially in the morning when I was supposed to be getting up. I continued this habit into adulthood, sleeping late whenever I got the chance. But this has, very gradually, changed. Now, a more normal pattern is that I jump up as soon as it is light, ready to go—maybe as early as 5:30/6:00 a.m. in the morning, and it is not uncommon for me to do a couple of hours work before breakfast. (I don't know if this is related to Vipassana but I also notice that I am much more interested in exercise and have even joined a gym, something that my earlier self would never have believed.)

In terms of relationships I have found some peace. I have a history of difficult, sometimes catastrophic, nearly always very dramatic, love relationships, which are often complicated, have taken up a lot of my energy, and brought me many tears. However, as with everything else these days, I am learning not to look for my happiness outside of myself and so have been able—even when things have been very bad on the outside—to remain happy within myself much more than in the past. Sometimes I do daydream about an impossible romance, or agonize over an unpromising relationship, but, perhaps because I am more self-aware, I catch myself at it much more quickly than I used to, and have the resource of Anapana and Vipassana now to help me to cut the daydreaming/agonizing short by focusing my attention on my breath or my sensations. It has been quite a relief to have had Vipassana on hand to help deal with this part of my life.

Accepting the ageing process has been one of the gains of meditation for Vajira, a professional dancer from Sri Lanka.

In my country people appreciate what I do and what I show. The standard of creative work, beautiful stories or dances, has made everyone happy and they look up to me to continue it, so I try my best even though I am not in peak form any more. I get others to keep it going, because the tradition also has to be preserved, otherwise it'll die. So, for my country I have to do that as long as I can, working part-time, practicing daily, but also teaching classes and doing stage work. With the practice of Vipassana, I understand and accept change—that my body can't do what I used to do in my early days. That has helped me not to greedily climb and try to maintain what I always did. It has made me more humble also, I don't crave publicity. There are other changes too. I became a vegetarian gradually and now my lifestyle is quieter. I just carry on my work because someone has to take over from me. I don't have any ambitions to become greater or anything like that. Now I am content . . . what I have done is enough.

❧

Meditation is a privileged moment that a person passes in calm far away from noise, far from everything! Particularly this tranquillity, which one finds so rarely in life. Life is a river which one purifies so little except in the course of meditation. It is sometimes peaceful, sometimes agitated, sometimes cloudy, sometimes dark. The mind is always overloaded with all sorts of thoughts. Meditation is an excellent way of taming the wandering mind. It is also a remedy for anger and melancholy.

—*Luc, age 13 from France*

❧

I think it's for everybody. The sooner they can learn the technique the better, even as children.

There may be people who will say, well I don't have any problems, why would I go and do this ten hard working days? For me, the fact they're saying that they don't need it is a very strong reason that they do. If they can just reflect inside themselves for a moment instead of listening to what the outside is telling them, they'll see. Go on now, ask yourself within, how is your life? How is your relationship? How is your work? Do you get angry? Do you get bad tempered? Do you get frustrated with other people and what they think and do and say? And if the reply to these is yes (and it's likely to be because that's how we human beings are), then the answer is yes, you do need the course.

—*In conversation, Michael Powell*
from Adelaide, Australia

❧

For Robert Johnson (USA), a former jail inmate, Vipassana is key to staying on track.

I won't stop this. I like meditation . . . not reacting in the everyday world . . . I'm developing ways to continue the practice of meditation in my life—how to make a wholesome living and be able to meditate. For the first time I'm able to say I don't like this situation, these kind of people, working here or there. With Vipassana I've got enough cushion to be able to tell if something's good or gonna turn out wrong for me. It's a challenge, how to develop a better lifestyle for myself. That's where the next level of personal work has been.

For a person in the jail house, if they have that sort of mind where they wish they could get some quiet, jails and prisons are noisy, people screaming out, gates slamming, somebody's yelling "Stand at attention!" and you get a chance to take Vipassana meditation, you should hop right on there . . . I'd tell anybody.

Now I know that this is the way
For the nonbeliever who wants to believe,
For the chronic faithless who secretly seeks faith.
This is the way for those who can never feel at ease
With partial human solutions like God, psychology,
    money.
It is for those who appreciate science
But cannot be comforted by it.
It's for the one who owns a thing because it works
Not because it has a brand name.
It's for those who will always cherish
A breath more than a word.

        —Ayelet Menahemi from Israel is a filmmaker. She
                sat her first Vipassana course in 1993 and
                          all the family now meditate.

The potential is unlimited. As a teacher of many ages, I feel that meditation should be an accepted daily occurrence for students of all generations. Vipassana gives everybody more peace, clarity, focus and self awareness. These skills are more important than math or science because they provide a person with an internal language of insight. They have also encouraged me to pursue artistic endeavors which no longer add to the misery of the world, but strive to enlighten, teach and inspire, to lift humanity upward!

—*Max Kiely, Canada*

It's given me a better idea of where, how and why we stand in the scheme of things and it's broadened my horizons. Instead of having such a narrow point of view, everything, it's all out there, so big. Brilliant!

I think I'm a bit more calm and a bit more compassionate. Not quite as locked into myself, you know. A bit of an opening, I think, I hope . . . .

I feel now I have a tool for expanding my awareness of where I'm headed in this life. It's the first time, and I've been looking for a long time—maybe 30 years and I've done a lot of reading—always knowing there is something else. This is the first time I've actually been able to find something that tells you how to do it. All the other things I've read are similar in terms of what you're trying to achieve but without telling you how and this tells you how.

I'm very glad I did it . . . yes very glad.

—*Post-course interviews with first-time students,*
Australia 1990.

May every reader find his or her path and grow in happiness and peace.

Appendix 1

VIPASSANA MEDITATION CENTERS

Typically information about Vipassana meditation spreads by word of mouth—someone attends a course, feels benefited and, wishing to share what they have gained, encourages family and friends to also attend. Interest in Vipassana and the demand for courses has grown dramatically in recent years and increasing numbers of people are now hearing about the technique through media reports, public talks, books and the internet.

The Vipassana website **http://www.dhamma.org** carries a comprehensive listing of ten-day residential courses that are being organized worldwide. Many of these retreats will be held at dedicated Vipassana centers, others at rented noncenter sites. A brief introduction to the technique and the code of discipline for courses are also available on the homepage. Application forms can either be completed on screen and emailed or printed off and sent to the course registrar. Information about Vipassana in a number of languages other than English can also be accessed via this website. In case of queries or particular requests, it's best to contact one of the centers directly. No previous knowledge or experience of meditation is needed to undertake the course, just a genuine desire to learn the technique and by doing one's own research, give it a fair trial.

There are many centers around the world regularly offering courses in Vipassana meditation as taught by S.N. Goenka, from India and Asia, through Australia and New Zealand, to Europe, Canada, USA and elsewhere.

Further information is available from the following centers:

Vipassana Meditation Center—*Dhamma Dharā*
P.O. Box 24
Shelburne Falls, MA 01370, USA
[1] (413) 625-2160; Fax: [1] (413) 625-2170
E-Mail: info@dhara.dhamma.org

Vipassana Meditation Center—*Dhamma Bhūmi*
P.O. Box 103
Blackheath, NSW 2785,
AUSTRALIA
[61] (2) 4787-7436, 4787-8431;
Fax: [61] (2) 4787-7221
E-Mail: info@bhumi.dhamma.org

Vipassana Center—*Dhamma Dīpa*
Harewood End; Hereford HR2 8JS,
UNITED KINGDOM
[44] (1989) 730-234; Fax: [44] (1989) 730-450
E-Mail: info@dipa.dhamma.org

Vipassana International Academy—*Dhamma Giri*
P.O. Box 6, Igatpuri 422 403, Dist. Nashik,
Maharashtra, INDIA
[91] (2553) 84076, 84086 or 84302;
Fax: [91] (2553) 4176
E-Mail: dhamma@vsnl.com

Appendix 2

MORE ABOUT VIPASSANA MEDITATION

Recommended books and tapes for the newcomer and where you can get them:

1. **The Art of Living: Vipassana Meditation as Taught by S.N. Goenka** by William Hart*

   A full-length study of the teaching of S.N. Goenka, prepared under his guidance and with his approval. It includes stories used on courses and answers to students' questions.

   Harper Collins, 1987, 170 pp.

   Reprinted in India by Vipassana Research Institute, Mumbai, 1988

   *Also available in Spanish, French, German, Hebrew, Farsi, Hindi, Marathi, Gujarati and Sindhi languages.

2. **The Discourse Summaries** by S.N. Goenka

   Summaries of the evening discourses from a ten-day Vipassana course, in which Mr Goenka provides a context and rationale for the actual practice of Vipassana meditation.

   Vipassana Research Institute, 1995

   *Full sets of discourses are also available on audio cassette tape in Spanish, French, Mandarin, Hindi, Gujarati, Farsi, Russian and Khmer languages.

3. **Meditation Now: Inner Peace through Inner Wisdom** by S.N. Goenka

   A collection of essays and interviews with Mr Goenka. This selection includes discourses originally delivered at the World Economic Forum at Davos, Switzerland, The Millennium

World Peace Summit at the UN and other essays addressing topics of contemporary concern.

Vipassana Research Publications, 2002, 128pp.

4. **Karma and Chaos** by Dr Paul Fleischman
New and collected essays (including **Why I Sit** and **The Therapeutic Action of Vipassana**) exploring the interface between psychiatry, science and the timeless teaching of the Buddha, from an eminent psychiatrist who practices and teaches Vipassana.

Vipassana Research Publications, 1999, 160pp.

5. **Cultivating Inner Peace** by Dr Paul Fleischman
The author holds up diverse examples of people who have inspired him in his personal quest for harmony and happiness. He includes an autobiographical account of his own experience with the practice of Vipassana.

Penguin Putnam, 1997, 300pp.

6. **The Buddha Taught Nonviolence, Not Pacifism** by Dr Paul Fleischman
A thought provoking essay and poem inspired by the terrorist attacks of September, 2001.

Pariyatti Press, 2002, 64pp.

7. **Art of Living, Audio Book** by William Hart with S.N. Goenka
In this audio tape version of the book, each chapter is read by the author, and following it is a story told by S.N. Goenka himself, taken directly from the talks he gives during a Vipassana course.

This is not a teach-yourself course for practicing Vipassana. Instead, it offers the listener a vivid picture of what it is like to practice Vipassana and what the technique can achieve.

Pariyatti Audio Editions, 1999, 4 tapes (5 hours total)

8. Introduction to Vipassana Video Tapes

Each of these tapes shows S.N. Goenka giving a public talk which describes the meditation technique and explains what is involved in undertaking a ten-day course.

(a) Long Introduction to Vipassana, (Australia 1990), 56 minutes.

(b) Short Introduction to Vipassana, (India 1988), 19 minutes, available in English and Hindi.

(c) Mental Wealth (U.S.A 2000), A public discourse given at the Harvard Business Club, New York, 62 minutes.

9. Doing Time, Doing Vipassana

Winner of the 1998 Golden Spire award at the San Francisco International Film Festival, this extraordinary documentary takes viewers into India's largest prison—known as one of the toughest in the world—and shows the dramatic change brought about by the introduction of Vipassana meditation.

Karuna Films, Ltd, 1997, 52 minutes.

10. Changing from Inside, produced and directed by David Donnenfield

This is a compelling account of an intensive pilot meditation program for inmates at a minimum security jail near Seattle, Washington.

Vipassana Research Publications, 1998, 42 minutes.

11. The Compass

This video from Karuna Films shows the benefits children have gained through the practice of Anapana meditation.

Vipassana Research Publications, 1999, 12 minutes.

12. Hill of Dhamma

This professionally produced film about a Vipassana meditation center was shot in India in 1995. Originally commissioned to be shown on Myanmar television, it was received with such enthusiasm by Western students that it has now been released for distribution worldwide.

Karuna Films, Ltd, 1995, 17 minutes.

Also available in Japanese or with Mandarin subtitles.

Sources for Obtaining Vipassana Publications

The following bookstores make books, videos and other publications available to those interested in Vipassana in this tradition. You may contact them directly for a list of current titles and their prices.

North America

PARIYATTI BOOK SERVICE
P.O. Box 15926
Seattle, Washington 98115 USA
[1](800) 829-2748; [1](206) 522-8175;
Fax [1](206) 522-8295
E-Mail; bookorders@pariyatti.com
On the web at www.pariyatti.com

Australia/New Zealand

DHAMMA BOOKS
P.O. Box 362
Blackheath
New South Wales 2785 AUSTRALIA
[61](2) 4787-5493; Fax: [61](2) 4787- 5393
E-mail: dhammabooks@alive.com.au
On the web at www.dhammabooks.com

VIPASSANA PUBLICATIONS AOTEAROA NZ
89 Mountain Road
Roturua NEW ZEALAND
[64](07) 348-7388; Fax: [64](07) 357-4372

Europe

INSIGHT BOOKS
 The Sun
 Garway Hill
 Herefordshire HR2 8EZ
 UNITED KINGDOM
 [44](0) 1981 580-436; Fax: [44](0) 1981 580-436
 E-mail: info@insightbooks.co.uk

AYANA BOOK SERVICE
 Bahnhofstr. 41/2
 D-78532 Tuttlingen GERMANY
 [49] (7461) 5148; Fax: [49](7461) 12443
 E-mail: contact@ayana-book.com
 On the web at www.ayana-book.com

India

THE BOOKSTORE
 Vipassana Research Institute
 Dhamma Giri
 P.O. Box 6
 Igatpuri 422 403
 District Nashik
 Maharashtra, INDIA
 [91](2533) 84076, 84086 or 84302;
 Fax: [91](2533) 84176